Dear Deb[...] [...] to
It is won[...] to
meet you & be in the
teacher training ~~Training~~
with you.
May you always cook
with spirit and live life
with great Spirit too!
Love & Warmest regards
Darlene
6·7·00

Cooking With Spirit

Making the Art
of Preparing and Sharing Good Food
a Spiritual Adventure

Cooking With Spirit

Making the Art
of Preparing and Sharing Good Food
a Spiritual Adventure

Darlene Jones

Lang Publishing
Portland, Oregon

Lang Publishing
6663 S.W. Beaverton Hillsdale Highway #105
Portland, Oregon 97225

*I dedicate this book to my loving family, friends, and students —
especially to my son, Greg Jones, and my daughter, Shannon Jones —
and to a few dear friends who have been very supportive of me
during the writing of this book, and in life in general in recent years,
Bob and Virginia Plainfield and Jeanette D'Amico.*

Acknowledgments

First I want to acknowledge my editor, Nancy Osa: Dear Nancy, without you there would be no book. What an incredible support you have been. My thanks to: Dr. Lynda Falkenstein for her perseverance and professional expertise in keeping me on track throughout this process; to Sheryl Mehary for her support and creative talents in designing this book; to Laura Swanson for her creative input and assistance in the early revision of this book, and for her unfailing support and friendship; to Ursula and Thorn Bacon, whose wisdom and professional insights were very helpful in guiding me through uncharted publishing waters; and to Leslie Temple Thurston, my teacher, to whom I owe a great deal of gratitude for the development of my inner being, especially the strength and persistence to continue this project through some very difficult times.

Without these special beings this project would not have been possible. Most of all, I give thanks to the mysteries of God, Goddess, All That Is for the guidance that You have given me, and continue to give me. I am humbled and gratified for all of the abundance You have presented to me.

Contents

Authors Note

Over the years, I have collected a file full of inspirational quotations, thoughts, and affirmations. They are the perfect accompaniment to Cooking with Spirit, and I'm pleased to share them with you in these pages. Inspiration being what it is, I don't always manage to hold onto a book title or an author's name. If, after all my best efforts, I have been unable to secure this information, I have credited the universal source: Anonymous. I've signed my own pearls of wisdom "D.J." May they guide your Spirit as they have mine.

— Darlene Jones

List of Abbreviations

cup	=	c.
ounce	=	oz.
package	=	pkg.
pint	=	pt.
pound	=	lb.
quart	=	qt.
tablespoon	=	Tbs.
teaspoon	=	tsp.

Introduction

Spirit: The Extra Ingredient

If you're like many people, cooking and entertaining seem to be more of a challenge than you normally have the courage (or energy!) to undertake. When you do muster the nerve to try, there often seems to be too much to do at once — *and something seems to be missing.*

You may struggle to put together a menu — what to serve, which foods go with what — then frantically fit in food shopping, advance preparations, spiffing up the house, and of course, the actual cooking and serving of the meal. By this time, you've forgotten that you are supposed to enjoy the process.

Fear not. I know how to find the missing ingredient that's been holding you back from the wondrous adventure of sharing good food in good company. *Cooking with Spirit* will help you to experience greater confidence and have more fun experimenting and cooking food — *and* sharing it with friends and family — with less stress and more energy than ever before. Welcome to my table.

This book combines two of my great passions — cooking and the Spirit. Since ancient times, a strong connection has existed between spirituality and the art of preparing and enjoying food. I perpetuate this relationship in my own cooking. Over the past twenty-five years, I have taught hundreds of people how to cook and enjoy a variety of ethnic dishes from around the globe. My instructions to them are always laced with spiritual philosophy and the positive aspects of learning anything new — especially the satisfaction of making and sharing great food.

Cooking with Spirit is more than just a collection of taste-pleasing, appealing-to-all-the-senses menus and recipes. It's a guide on how to integrate cooking with care into our lives, and the lives of our loved ones. My students, family, and friends have experienced this "something extra" in my cuisine — my combination of Spirit and food. What great times we've had at classes, parties, and gatherings; conversing, telling stories, singing around the table for hours. No one ever wants to leave! The food and wine were appreciated, sure, but it's the element of connection that makes a meal memorable. It's all about the people in our lives, and the body, mind, Spirit connection.

For me, the process of cooking and sharing has become a spiritual involvement that enhances and enriches my life more than I ever thought possible. I realize that my passionate attitude toward food and the people I serve helps my guests feel good about themselves. To share love, memories, ideas, laughter, and even intimate feelings over great food and drink is truly the essence of life.

Joining with others around a table laden with good, wholesome, elegant food is a bonding experience that many of us have lost in our busy, fragmented society. Families rarely eat meals together anymore without rushing to get to the next job, meeting, or practice. I invite you to pause; take a breath. *Cooking With Spirit* is a means of reclaiming the richness and quality of our lives by making time for others in an intimate dining experience, whether we share it with two or twenty people.

Over my cooking and traveling lifetime, people and the places that they come from have inspired my appetites. You will find many of their stories at the heart of some of my food memories, which I share with you here. I hope you'll enjoy hearing of my own connections as you learn to add that "extra ingredient" to your cooking experience. May they inspire you as they have me.

Chapter One

Creating a Dinner Party

What bounty! The foods we eat are both sustenance and among the great joys and pleasures of life. Making the human connection over a nourishing meal benefits body and soul. You'll find that adding spirit to your kitchen creations is a healing process, not only for the cook but for all of those gathered around the table as well.

In ancient times, food was an integral part of religious ceremonies. Festivals might stretch into several days, filled with gossip, games, food, and intimate rendezvous of all kinds. Worshippers brought food to the temple altars for their Gods, everything from sheaves of wheat to slaughtered lambs. They offered these gifts of food to please and appease the Gods, and to request special favors.

We have come a long way from those ancient times, sometimes for the better, and sometimes for the worse … Today our food "comes from" supermarkets where most of the items that we purchase are packaged up tightly so that we cannot touch them, smell them, or closely examine them. Often, we have little or no idea where the food we buy was grown, how it was fertilized, whether it was sprayed with pesticides, when it was harvested, or how long it has been sitting on the shelf or out of refrigeration. Because of these factors, there is a growing trend toward "organics" — foods that are certified to be grown without harmful substances. They are increasingly available at your local supermarket, and of course, at specialty organic produce markets.

Start with Spirit

Our thoughts, attitudes, and knowledge affect the foods that we prepare and of which we partake. Our cooking and eating experience depends on how we view the food from the start. All too often a trip to the market seems like such a large chore that we overlook the beauty of fresh produce — the gorgeous colors, the variety, and the sheer bountifulness that we in the Western Hemisphere are so fortunate to have. Going to the market to buy our food should be a wonderfully gratifying experience. Start with that thought, and a certain respect and appreciation will grow from it.

"Work is love made visible. And if you cannot work with love but only with distaste, it is better that you should leave your work and sit at the gate of the temple and take alms of those who work with joy. For if you bake bread with indifference, you bake a bitter bread that feeds but half our hunger."
— *The Prophet,* Kahlil Gibran

Bringing home our food and unwrapping it, storing it, and preparing it is really a creative and enjoyable adventure. Think of the hundreds of ways a specific food or ingredient can be prepared, not to mention which ethnic variety you might favor on any given day! The complete process appeals to all of our senses. Take a moment to enjoy it.

When we are aware, we delight in the aromas, tastes, and all the different sensations and textures, as well as the visual beauty of a meal. These things feed our spirit, which in turn nurtures our cooking. We can make the most basic food taste delicious by how we think of it, how we prepare it, and how we serve it.

We all know that anything tastes better when it's served beautifully. Even a simple sandwich tastes better when served on a pretty, garnished plate, alongside a bowl of fruit or fresh flowers as a centerpiece. This is what cooking with spirit is all about. Going the extra mile to set a lovely table, light candles, and polish the silver is very nurturing to yourself, and to the friends and family with whom you choose to share your dinner. They will truly appreciate your effort and be healed by the whole event.

Sometimes we're reluctant to open up and entertain people, and it comes from the base feeling of fear. You must have the courage to conquer your fear and invite people into your home anyway. Remember, the real human hunger is for love and acceptance, not just sustenance.

The fact is, we need each other, but we seem to be in denial. In order to overcome this, we must come from love within our own minds, and then this will project out, drawing love back to us. Start by enveloping your mind in love; acknowledge the fear you feel, and then change it to loving thoughts. When you do that, your love will move naturally outward into the universe, and you will *want* to share it. One way to do that is to connect with others around the dining room table, whether for a simple, intimate repast or a large, gregarious celebration.

Take the plunge! Give — give in the best way you know how. It doesn't have to be out of the ordinary at all. It will be enough! Whatever you do that comes from your heart and your spirit will be enough. We want things to be perfect, but that's not the point at all. When your guests leave happy and relaxed, you will all feel a sense of joy and accomplishment. Preparing and partaking of a meal with all the trimmings is a creative learning adventure that brings pleasure and satisfaction to everyone who comes to the table.

Choosing Your Guests

To keep a positive outlook, choose to entertain people that you love, or at least like. If you "must" entertain people you don't like or maybe don't even know, find a reason to enjoy them and the whole process anyway. You can *guide* your thoughts and attitudes.

You may feel that you *must* entertain mean, old Aunt Mary or your spouse's boss whom you hardly know, but you do have some *choice* in the matter. Here are some of the things I do to ready my spirit prior to entertaining anyone at all:

- use the time to prepare a new dish or menu that I've wanted to make for a long time.
- take a bubble bath with candlelight and meditate for twenty to thirty minutes prior to party time.
- during meditation or while preparing dinner, visualize my guests with a warm, glowing light around them and think very good thoughts about them before their arrival.
- invite as many dynamic people with positive energy, whom I love being with, and have fun myself!

How do I accomplish this? The magic word is *attitude*.

It is a person's attitude at the beginning of a task that, more than anything else, will effect a successful outcome. We are interdependent. It is impossible to succeed without others. And our attitudes toward others will determine their attitudes toward us.

So, as you prepare for your dinner party emotionally, guide your thoughts with these positive ideas. I will:

- do my best to find the sense of humor in this experience and to consciously lighten up and not take the whole thing so seriously.
- see this time as an adventure and a new learning experience.
- understand that I am in a giving mode and that "what goes around comes around."
- be loving and accepting of everyone who enters my home.

Human beings' deepest craving is to be needed — to feel important and appreciated. Give it to them and they'll return the favor to you. Try this for the next thirty days: Treat everyone with whom you come in contact as the most important person on earth. If you do this for a month, you'll do it for the rest of your life, and benefit by it in a big way.

"of love be more careful than anything else."
— e. e. cummings

Planning the Menu

People say to me, "How do you do it?" Meaning, the cooking, the artistry, the ambiance. I tell them it's what I love to do, so it's effortless. It's simple, but it's not always easy. Or it's easy, but not always simple. Creating in this way is a challenge that I embrace. My desire comes from the heart, it comes from creative energy, deep down inside. It comes from spirit.

I don't spend hours on meals to impress anyone or to be "better than." I do it because an urge deep down inside calls me to create in this way. This undeniable something is our core — it is what we are truly about. I pay diligent attention to this energy and treat it with care and respect. Some people call it the small, quiet (sometimes insistent) voice within.

The voice says: "I wonder what such and such would taste like together." Or, "It's spring-time, wouldn't asparagus soup taste delicious right now?" Or, "What a cold rainy, dreary weekend; I think I'll make a big pot roast, or spaghetti and meatballs." Or, "Summer! It reminds me of when I was in Spain at one of those wonderful, late-night, outdoor restaurants in Madrid. I think I'll make paella this weekend." Spirit is talking to me, recalling past positive experiences and creating new ones in the present.

And so it begins. Listen to your inner voice, and consider the details: Take into account how the food will look. A contrast in color is very important. Visualize how the meal will look on the table, buffet, and on each individual plate. You don't want everything on the plate to look bland. If you're serving chicken breasts with herbed rice, don't serve cauliflower or corn or white beans with them. Try green beans and broiled tomatoes Provençal instead. Visualize!

Now, with whom do you wish to share this fabulous dinner? You've been wanting to introduce Betsy and Paul to each other. Invite them. The Andrews and the Mitchells would really complement this group. Invite them, too. Caring and sharing with people we love — that is spirit manifested in a life experience.

Sometimes your inner voice speaks more spontaneously. You may pick up and arrange an especially gorgeous bunch of flowers or seasonal vegetables. It looks so spectacular, you'll decide to plan a dinner around it! Invite some friends over on the spur of the moment. Ask them to bring some wine or light hors d'oeuvres, and the party begins.

When you've thought everything through, *write down your menu* — from the appetizers to coffee and tea. Keep it handy as you track down all the recipes you will need. Then make your shopping list. Go through each recipe, beginning with the hors d'oeuvres and ending with the dessert. That way there is less chance of forgetting anything. When I write out my list of needed ingredients, I group grocery items, dairy products, fresh produce, and meats separately on the page. This saves time and confusion at the market. After you've made your food list, plan the centerpiece for your table and add any items you need for that to the list as well.

Be sure to consider your time constraints, budget, and expertise as you go along. Think about preparing some of the dishes ahead, if possible (more on this later.) The more you can prepare ahead, the better. Now you're ready to go shopping, a process that puts you into motion. It's all part of spirit. What fun!

Some of the menus in this book are lengthy. Don't feel that you have to prepare all of the recipes in them. If dinner is spur-of-the-moment, without a lot of time beforehand, ask your friends to bring one or two dishes. People enjoy helping in this way — they love to be "in on it." Just have them bring simple things that they don't have to fuss over too much. Remember, this dinner was *your* idea, not theirs.

With the process underway, the work begins to flow. The energy builds, the plan unfolds, and so much gets done … easily and joyfully! The shopping, the preparation, and the table — along with the actual cooking — fulfill the experience. Finally, orchestrating a social event around the whole meal is an art form that is all spirit.

As you begin, think about:

- Time
- Cost and budget
- The season
- Style of menu; such as French, Italian, Thai, Chinese, Mexican, American, or a combination of different ethnic foods (blending a menu).
- Centerpieces, decorations, etc.
- Choosing guests

Make Ahead Dishes

Many dishes can be prepared days, sometimes weeks, ahead of the event that you're hosting, which frees up your time on that busy day. Keep prepared food refrigerated or frozen until just before needed. My recipes will tell you whether to defrost or bring food to room temperature, or to bake dishes straight from the freezer, etc.

Remember that when foods are cold, the flavors are masked and less intense than when warm or hot. Taste the dish, and season accordingly. Many casseroles, along with most prepared desserts, freeze well. Again, check each recipe for specific reheating instructions, and use the frozen items within the designated period of time.

Timesaver: When preparing a dish just a day or so ahead of time, place it directly into the serving dish or platter and cover them well. Then they can be used right on the table.

It's perfectly permissible to buy dessert or some tabbouli salad from your local deli to go with your own spanakopita and Greek salad. You still get to be creative and nourish those you love, and not kill yourself in the process. What a concept!

"At the root we are all very much alike, but we have different symptoms so that we do not bore each other to tears at parties."
— *The Tao of Love,* Ivan Hoffman

Serving Dishes

I have had fun over the years collecting interesting serving pieces of every size, shape, and material imaginable — glass, plastic, brass, silver, pewter, shells, woven baskets and trays, old boxes, trophies, wood — you name it. For serving purposes, these may be lined with napkins, tablecloths, paper doilies, interesting paper, or organic leaves such as lettuce, cabbage, grape — even some large stems of tropical foliage from your garden or the florist. Be sure to rinse foliage well to remove any pesticides or other foreign substances.

Table Decorations and Centerpieces

Find new ways to combine and display the usual flowers or fruits as centerpieces. Float a single flower or two in a large bowl of water, and surround the "pond" with votive candles or floating candles. A large urn filled with bright red, shiny apples in the fall can look spectacular. Add a bunch of red candles, and serve something "apple-y" in the meal for extra drama … like apple crisp, apple pie, baked apples, apples in the salad or in the main dish. After the apples have ripened somewhat, make apple sauce with them, eat, freeze, or take some to a friend. This arrangement is edible!

And don't underestimate the artistic possibilities of vegetables. They are so beautiful whole, sitting in a bowl or on a large platter in bunches. Sometimes I cut fruit or vegetables in half — the patterns inside of them are fascinating, and their seeds or stones add visual texture as well. Picture one of your favorite baskets filled with big, leafy cabbages or squash. I often fill a large, antique urn with ornate handles on either side with artichokes. Then I use napkins in that same artichoke-green color for a dramatic effect. In season, these "centerpiece" foods can be far less expensive than flowers, and besides they're recyclable … you can make soups, salads, or pâtés and hors d'oeuvres with them. Be sure to keep the centerpiece low enough so that your guests can see each other across the table.

Exhibit your own objets d'art. A beautiful ceramic or porcelain bowl that can stand alone makes a wonderful center-piece framed by long-stemmed, tapered candles in a comple-mentary color. Masses of candles in candlesticks of various heights can be striking and dramatic all by themselves.

If you're giving a buffet party for the summer sailing

"Live in the present.
Do the things you know need to be done.
Do all the good you can each day.
The future will unfold."
— Peace Pilgrim

crew, use your model sailboat as a centerpiece. Add some natural shells and, voila, you're done! Again, think about what you love, or what your guest of honor loves, and use that as your theme for decorations and centerpieces that are uniquely appropriate to the occasion. Let your inner spirit and passion be expressed in this way.

When You're Too Busy To Do It All

If time is your scarce resource, for a really easy dessert, buy a good-quality ice cream and serve it with a fresh fruit sauce. All you need are fresh berries or other fruit; whirl them in a food processor with some sugar and flavoring, like vanilla or liquor. Or serve the ice cream with chocolate sauce *and* the homemade fruit sauce, plus some toasted, chopped nuts. One of my favorite toppings is praline sauce; I've included the recipe in this book (see Gelati and Pecan Praline Sauce.)

Still too much effort? End your meal with a fruit and cheese board, scattered with a few good chocolates. Whenever you make a more elaborate dessert, double the recipe and freeze one batch to serve later. Then you can take it out in time for your party and make the schedule easier on YOU.

You don't have to sacrifice taste and quality. Some great takeouts, besides most desserts, are mixed vegetables salads and whole, roasted chicken. Many supermarkets offer spit-cooked chickens. They are delicious and can be dressed up with your own roasted vegetables, pastas, rice, or taken on a quick, impromptu picnic. Just add some fresh, sliced tomatoes, good baguette bread, fresh fruit, and cheese, and the picnic fare is done. These ideas and combinations are delicious, high-quality, and simple to assemble.

Another time-saving picnic menu includes a Tupperware container full of cold Shrimp Gazpacho, pocket bread (either plain or toasted under the broiler briefly) spread with hummus or baba ganouzh, some raw almonds, grapes, and sliced melons, and a couple of your favorite cheeses and chocolate chip cookies, homemade or store-bought. Easy and simple, these foods look and taste great together, and they are healthy and delicious. *And* they won't break the bank either, especially if you make some or all of the menu yourself.

Providing a Nurturing Atmosphere

Once you have taken care of the food, pour your energy into setting the scene. The idea is to make your home surroundings as pleasant as possible — not too cluttered, but adorned with things that make YOU and others feel good. Things that nurture you and let people see who you are. Your divine, creative self.

Remember to include the four basic, universal elements as food for your spirit:

Earth	Air
Water	Fire

Reflect these nurturing elements in your home to the best of your ability by displaying them in your environment.

The Joy of Creating
"Force yourself to smile and you'll soon stop frowning.
Force yourself to laugh and you'll soon find something to laugh about."
— Anonymous

Earth: Plants, flowers, fruits, vegetables, rocks — display them to visually please YOU. Be conscious of what pleases you and feeds your spirit and why — then surround yourself with these things.

Air: The aroma of candles and flowers fills the air with negative ions, which feed your spirit. Use essential oils with light-bulb rings or aromatherapy diffusers found at health food or gift stores — or burn some incense or a smudge stick. Weather permitting, open doors and windows and let the smell of fresh air in, the sounds of birds chirping, the wind, and the trees' rustling response. Be consciously aware of nature in this simple but gratifying way. Breathe deeply, filling your lungs with fresh air. Relax and melt into the air. Most of us do not breathe deeply enough nor are conscious of the fact that without our next breath we could not survive. Be thankful and grateful for the air that you breathe.

Water: A small waterfall in your house, or a bowl of water with rocks in it, or a bowl of water with flowers or leaves floating in it is very soothing and beautiful to look at. Consider a waterfall or pond for your garden, and dine outdoors. The sound of water is very soothing and energy-giving.

Fire: In the autumn, winter, and spring, light a fire in your fireplace often. If you don't have a fireplace, light candles. Not only when you are entertaining, but just for yourself, perhaps next to you as you're reading or watching a movie. Or turn out all the lights and light several aromatherapy candles in your favorite scents.

Make your front-door entrance look appealing. It's the first impression and "mood" builder that your guests — and you — will see. Inside, dust and vacuum for YOU, and for your guests. Clean is comfortable. If you live in a dusty area, think about using air purifiers. If you live in a very noisy area, think of building or buying a small waterfall to enhance your sound environment.

Surround yourself and your guests with flowers, green plants, water bowls, fire, candles, sumptuous fabrics and colors, and beautiful books and magazines. Set the tone with uplifting music — rock, vocals, meditative instrumentals, nature sounds; whatever suits your fancy.

To become more aware of how our surroundings affect us, positively and negatively, read a book on Feng Shui (pronounced Foong Shway), "the Chinese art of placement." Feng Shui helps you arrange your home in the most harmonious way possible.

Decorating the Table

"Linens" can consist of everything from bare wood to place mats, tablecloths, lace, golden fabric, table runners, etc. I once went to a gourmet picnic where fresh turf was laid out on all the outdoor tables instead of tablecloths. Again, let your creativity be your guide.

There are literally hundreds of ways to decorate your table. You will find plenty of literature on how to properly set a table with china, glasses, and cutlery. Instead, I want to give you a few examples of how to dress up the table in a festive way that will express your spirit and complement your dinner — whether casual or formal. My favorite way to carry out a theme is with party gifts and favors.

It's always fun to give gifts as well as to receive them. I find it challenging and creative to come up with special and different favors for a dinner party. This is not a must for all of your gatherings, but when the mood strikes or when your theme cries for something special, favors are a wonderful, extra luxury of giving.

Place a favor at each place setting. Some inexpensive ideas:

- A special poem, quote, or saying written on parchment paper, rolled up, and tied with a colored ribbon, straw, cord, etc., that matches your table theme or color. Place one on the plate or napkin of each place setting.

- A picture that you took at a prior gathering that included the individual guest or whole group there. Seal in a color-coordinated envelope with each person's name written on the front in gold or silver ink.

- Dried or fresh bundles of herbs from your garden, wrapped in your favorite way, or displayed in a little, decorative glass jar.

- Baby pumpkins in autumn, set among fall colors and decorations. Write a guest's name on each and use as place cards.

- Bud vases in front of each place with one gorgeous flower from your garden in it — these become the table decoration. You may add a collectable to the center and/or candles. Invite your guests to take their flowers home with them when they leave. Roses, dahlias, camellias, irises, peonies, tulips, rhododendrons, etc. are some flowers that cut well and travel well. They look spectacular grouped together on a table in this way.

- A jar of bubbles to blow at the party and then take home. (I keep a jar of bubbles in a kitchen drawer to blow when I am taking myself too seriously!) They are an instant mood modifier.

- A little bag of roasted nuts, perhaps, which you made for the hors d'oeuvres as well, tied with a pretty ribbon. Include a copy of the recipe tied with the ribbon, printed on colored paper that matches your table decor.

- Any other small, homemade food items that travel well make nice, personal favors to give your guests as a remembrance of a warm, loving shared evening.

  Some theme-inspired favors:

- Mardi Gras time — colorful plastic beads from the dime store to wear as leis around your necks.

- Fourth of July — little American flags and a rolled up copy of the Declaration of Independence. (When did you read it last?)

- Christmas — candies, a red or green candle wrapped with a holly branch, or a colorful ornament.

- Seafood Dinner — small bowl of goldfish or a beautiful shell for each guest at their place setting.

- Indian Dinner — *bindis* for all the women to wear (bindis are the exotic red dots or ornamental jewels worn in the middle of the forehead by East Indian women. Buy the self-adhesive kind at an East Indian shop.) Men love to see them on women!

- Mexican Dinner — a big, bright paper flower that matches your piñata centerpiece.

- Asian Dinner — Red is always a good theme color, because that's the money color in Chinese lore. Pack individually wrapped Asian candies — ginger, herb, green tea, all kinds of flavors! — in small ceramic rice bowls or lacquered tea cups. Or offer bamboo tea strainers tied together with packets of green tea, or sushi trays full of candies or fortune cookies, all wrapped up in cellophane with a big, red bow. Browse an Asian specialty store for paper puppets, hand-painted chopsticks, or Asian fans, from paper to silk.

♥   ♥   ♥

True, not all of us have the time or the inclination to make our own favors. If you do, that's great. If not, instead you can visualize and research how to present your dinner or entertainment concepts, and then use the goods and services available to you to make them a reality. Purchased favors need not be

"Art is food for the soul."

— D.J.

expensive, and may be less costly than making them yourself, because often time is money. And it's the thought that counts!

Hospitality and the Social Graces

In every relationship that you nurture in life, your attitude and behavior will "make or break" the connection. Thinking and acting hospitably — with a generous and receptive spirit — nourishes you as well as everyone else. When you are in touch with your spirit, it affects everything that you do and everyone who comes into your life, so make your associations the best!

Hospitality is the art of welcoming people into your home and your life, and making them feel comfortable. It is practiced out of respect, never condescension, in an honest desire to connect with people. Your hospitable attitude not only makes guests feel at home, but lifts them up and lightens them. They forget about the stresses of life, and feel a freedom to relax and have fun. Spirit is present and permeates the surroundings. A friend of mine explains it thus: "The angels were there." Sometimes everything just clicks, and "the angels are there" because you're coming from your spirit. That's what turns a gathering into a memorable party.

When I think about entertaining, *kind* and *gracious* are the words that come to my mind. As you open the door at the arrival of your guests, they become your main concern. Treat them like royalty. Help them to feel comfortable by breaking the ice with introductions. Make sure everyone is included in conversation. By the way, the word "conversation" means a two-way experience, as I used to tell my children. You talk, then they talk, then you talk, then they talk. Be aware of this in your conversations. Be a good listener. If you're a really good listener, you never interrupt anyone — that's the real test!

But, as host, you create the group dynamic. Ask questions to draw quiet guests out. Hold your own opinions, and respect others' opinions as well. Be curious and interested in other people; that's the highest form of compliment.

Two more things are very important — a really good sense of humor, and being real, not ostentatious in any way. People like and are attracted to people who are *really* themselves. So, "Know thyself," and let your guests see the real you — and make the spiritual connection.

"The food and every-thing else are only acces-sories to the relationships, which become treasured experiences. This is about bonding, which we need more of in our fragmented culture."

— D.J.

Basic Social Etiquette

We are becoming a much more open and casual society, which I think is a good thing. So unless you are creating a very formal, protocol-type affair, keep your introductions simple. For a formal situation, do a little advance research via the numerous books (or the Internet) on social etiquette.

For example, a simple "Laura, this Rich. Rich, this is Laura" is perfectly fine. If someone of the clergy or a high political office is present, I introduce them more formally as a matter of respect:

"Reverend Johnson, I would like you to meet my friend Melissa."
Or, "Mrs. Clinton, I would like you to meet Mr. Smith."

The important thing is to introduce strangers to each other *right away, FIRST THING*. So many times people forget to do this, and an awkwardness sets in immediately. Who needs that!

At a large gathering it's a good idea to introduce a new arrival to several people, say four or five, before leaving them alone, so the new guest has a level of comfort and isn't a stranger. When you are the guest, it is up to you to circulate and meet different people at a function. These days, it's called networking or "schmoozing." As either host or guest, some of the ways to move on to others that I use are:

"It's been great talking with you …"
"Now if you'll excuse me, I'd like to meet some of the other guests."
"It's very nice to meet you. I hope we get to meet again."
Or, "Let's get together next week."

Introduction Basics:

Always make introductions when meeting someone for the first time. If the other person does not introduce herself to you, introduce yourself to her.

At the table, men should pull chairs out for women. (This isn't sexist, just a nice gesture.)

The very first action after you sit down should be to place the napkin on your lap by draping it loosely in a casual way. Do not totally shake it out. Use a subtle, graceful gesture that does not draw attention to the action.

While eating, wait to speak until after you swallow your food, and chew with your mouth closed.

In conversation, be conscious of asking questions and being a good listener, as well as telling interesting stories yourself.

For family-style dining, where the food is served at the table from bowls and platters, passing from left to right has always been the rule. It just makes sense to have everything going in one direction.

When you prepare individual plates in the kitchen, serve each person on the right and take away the plate afterwards from the left.

When you leave the table, place your napkin to the left of your place setting — unfolded, just draped.

The day after a party or gathering, *ALWAYS* call your hosts to thank them, or send a thank-you note in the mail.

♥ ♥ ♥

Social Graces Review:

* Maintain good eye contact when speaking to someone.

* Stand when another person enters the room.

* Learn to shake hands firmly — not bone-crushing and not like a limp dishrag. People can tell a great deal about you by your handshake.

* *Please* and *thank you* are a must.

* Cultivate being a good listener.

* Be on time.

* When passing in front of someone, say "Excuse me."

* Don't interrupt other conversations.

* Don't broadcast personal problems; it probably won't help you — it cannot help others.

* Don't talk about your health unless it's good — or unless you're talking to your doctor.

* Dress for dinner, even if that just means wearing a clean shirt or a pair of earrings.

♥ ♥ ♥

"It is more important to be interested than interesting. You learn much more that way."

— D.J.

Lighting and Music

Music and soft light are very supportive to your spirit, building a positive feeling of hospitality. Lighting needs to be flattering to everyone, so don't keep the lights too bright. You want to be able to see the food and each guest through a soft, warm glow of light. At the table, I prefer very dim electric light, plus candles to elegantly light everything — the result is very flattering and gives a peaceful ambiance. So, dim the lights and use as many of your candles as are needed.

When I'm entertaining, I like appropriate background music. It's fun to play music from the country that inspired the menu — Italian opera or pop with an Italian menu; a French chanteuse with French food; Ricky Martin with a Latin-American dinner, for example. Use your imagination!

Classical music of any kind that appeals to you is always a good choice. Jazz is pleasant during the cocktail hour, which by the way, should not exceed one hour. Themes from some films make good background music, as well as instrumentals or solos by artists such as Frank Sinatra, Nancy Wilson, Barbra Streisand, Natalie and Nat King Cole, Kenny G., Yanni, John Tesh, or Harry Connick Jr. Nature music works well also — sounds of water and birds, chimes, etc. Just remember that while eating, soft and calming is best. Sometimes while we are relaxing at the table, after enjoying a satisfying meal, I like to "zip up" the music a bit, making it more conducive to perking everyone up for lively conversation and stories, or even sing-alongs.

Be yourself! Entertain in the manner that you feel most comfortable. Reflect your own lifestyle and do it to the best of your ability, and your friends and family will love all that you do. Feed your spirit and others by being creative. It is important that you, as the host, have FUN at your own party. Remember, it's all a matter of attitude!

Nurturing Yourself before Your Guests Arrive

Taking time out for yourself is a very important part of the "giving" process. You DESERVE this! When all of your party preparations are in place, take a breather:

- Retire to your special room, draw the shades, light incense or candles (preferably aromatherapy), and meditate for at least twenty minutes. You may want to add your favorite meditative music, instrumental, chanting, nature sounds, or whatever.

- Make sure to take off your shoes and put your feet up.

- Take several deep breaths. My favorite breathing technique: Breathe in for 7 counts, hold for 28 counts, breathe out for 14 counts; do this 7 times. This takes some practice, and is very healing. Then meditate for twenty to thirty minutes .

"Your Spirit is the heart and soul of who you are. Nurture it daily. Honor it and never let it go."

— D.J.

- Visualize your guests, and surround them with golden light and bless each one of them.

- Take a long bubble bath with your favorite drink at tub-side. Light several candles and turn out all other lights. Play soft, meditative music. Nibble at a bowl of grapes or a sliced apple as you soak.

- Sit in a chair and read about your favorite subject for twenty to thirty minutes. Or page through your favorite magazine — just for you, just for fun, with no goal in mind at all.

- Sit in a comfy chair with your feet up and write ten things that you love about yourself. I know this is hard, but do it anyway! Or write ten affirmations that you are working on at the present time instead.

- Gaze at something in nature, in total silence for fifteen to twenty minutes.

And now, before you head for the kitchen, I have a few words about self-image — and calories, eating, gaining and losing weight. Like many people, I've been on "diets" for much of my life. I found out a secret: they don't work. Balance, in food and drink as in everything else in life, is the key. Not too much, and not too little. After all this time, I have learned that moderation is the only diet for me. While "diet foods" don't work for me; real, wholesome, nourishing food that really sustains me does. When the food is beautifully served and tastes really good, I find I need smaller amounts.

At the same time, I have learned to appreciate and respect my body as it is. We have an inner knowing of what is best for us. If we take good care of our bodies — exercise, eat and drink in moderation, and get plenty of rest — we will realize with some satisfaction that our size is our size, and terrific just the way it is. What a relief! We can shine just the way we are. Keep this in mind as you prepare to indulge for the evening. Again, you deserve it!

♥ ♥ ♥

"Praying is talking to God, but meditating is listening to God."

Chapter Two

Food and Spirit from Around the World

I have been very fortunate to have traveled all over the world. To a great degree, my connection with people and their diverse cultures focused around the food they prepared. I saw that the way in which we prepare and eat our food in different parts of the world fosters our customs and our spirit connection.

Climate dictates how people cook and eat their food. Many people live and cook primarily outdoors because it's too hot indoors. They may not eat dinner until the sun goes down and the air is cooler and more conducive to sitting around a picnic table, partaking of their evening meal. In Asian cultures near the equator, people cook outside on braziers, or charcoal under a grill, right out in the open. It makes sense that most of their foods would be stir-fried or deep fried or barbecued; these cooks don't use ovens. Though they may lack leavened breads of any kind, the hilly land is perfect for growing rice, so a pot or steamer basket of rice works as the meal's accompaniment.

Inhabitants of some warm-climate countries, such as Spain and Italy, may enjoy a lengthy lunch followed by a siesta. Then they'll work till eight P.M. and eat dinner around nine or ten, or even later. As these Western European cultures become "globalized," their customs have begun to change. However, it takes a long time for such age-old customs — especially those associated with food and spirit — to disappear.

With the spread of business and leisure travel, television, computers, and literature, the world has become smaller, and I find that we in the United States are "blending" more and more of the foods of other cultures with our own. An exchange is also taking place as other countries embrace "American" food. I think we are getting the better end of the deal here! A fast-food burger can hardly compare to handmade pasta with a wonderful sauce or grilled Greek lamb on a skewer.

Through many years of traveling, I have taken notes and brought home recipes and menus from afar, and adapted them to my way of living and local supermarket offerings. The following menus feature some of my favorite foods from around the world. I have taught my cooking students how to make them, and updated them over the years when necessary. Food goes in and out of style like almost everything else. I have simplified technique, streamlined some of the more difficult recipes so that they can be prepared in much less time, and in many cases have cut down on fat content as well.

I hope you'll enjoy sampling from this collection of menus from around the world, and that you'll be moved to include family and friends in the experience. Come along with me as we begin our *Cooking with Spirit* journey in Italy, then delve into French cuisine, cruise the Mediterranean, savor the flavors of Asia, and find ourselves back in the familiar territory of North America, with tastes from Mexico and the Pacific Northwest. Let's go!

Chapter Three

Italy

If anyone has spirit, it's the Italian people. They do everything with great flair, artistry, and passion. From architecture, art, textiles, and fashions to fabulous food and wine, their spirit shines through second to none. If I had to choose another county to live in, it would be Italy. Their culture has affected my own expression of spirit more than any other place I have visited.

Venice is my favorite city in Italy and in the world — the romance of the islands surrounded by water, the beautiful architecture, the hospitality of the Italian people … It's a joy to be in Venice — there's an illusion of what is real and what isn't. At every turn you see a new scene: You may be walking along a street built of huge stones with a solid feel to it, and you turn a corner and find water; you realize that you're on an island — you're not at all on terra firma. Venice was uniquely built on a spiritual concept, the dream of building this city on many islands. Who would have ever thought such a thing possible? This enthusiasm is reflected in the region's cooking. It's a magical place to me.

Italian Menu #1:

Dinner in a Venetian Palazzo

Crostini with Pesto and Smoked Ham
Red Pepper Salad with Sun Dried Tomatoes and Olives
Curried Risotto Venezia with Shrimp and Asparagus
Zuccotto with Raspberry Sauce

On one memorable birthday in Venice, my partner hired a gondola and accordion player and we set out for a sail along the Grand Canal as the sun went down. We floated along the canal, sipping champagne from stem glasses, and when the accordion player played "Happy Birthday," we all started singing. Everyone on the canal could hear us — the people hanging off the vaporettos going home from work, the tourists in the streets, the people in the other gondolas — and they all started singing "Happy Birthday to Darlene." It was quite amazing, to say the least.

Back at our hotel, we invited our gondolier and the accordion player to join us at our table in a beautiful, very dark, tapestry-filled dining room, and we enjoyed a risotto with curry like nothing I'd ever tasted before. What a spiritual feeling to share a glass of wine and some dessert with the gondolier and the accordion player on that special evening.

I worked hard to recreate this meal, which I've shared with many friends and students since then. Each time, I relive that birthday celebration, and my guests share joyously in the experience.

Crostini with Pesto and Smoked Ham

Italians love their grilled breads with a never-ending list of toppings. We in the U.S. have adopted them — much to our taste buds' delight. Crostini is easy to prepare and the toppings and combinations of ingredients are as limitless as your imagination. Top the toasts with roasted red pepper, sun-dried tomatoes, cooked shrimp, or a piece of marinated artichoke heart. It's fun to offer a variety toppings.

Serves 6. May double or triple.

Pesto:

2 c.	loosely packed fresh basil leaves
1/2 c.	extra-virgin olive oil
1	large clove garlic
1 tsp.	salt
	Freshly ground black pepper to taste
2 Tbs.	pine nuts
1/2 c.	Parmesan cheese

Bread and Ham:

12 slices	good baguette bread, or other substantial French or Italian bread
2 to 3 oz.	thinly sliced smoked ham, julienned (see "My Way," below)

Small, whole basil leaves, for garnish

1. Make the pesto: In food processor place the basil, 1/4 c. olive oil, garlic, salt, and pepper. Process until this becomes a saucelike mixture, slowly adding the remaining oil until puréed. Then add the pine nuts and blend lightly. (I like the pine nuts to be chunky in the pesto.) Transfer to a small bowl and mix in the cheese. Set pesto aside.
2. Grill the bread slices over medium heat in a lightly oiled frying pan until golden. Or toast in oven on a cookie sheet sprayed with olive oil (also spray the bread on each side) at 350 degrees for about 10 to 20 minutes, until lightly crisp and golden.
3. Spread each piece of bread liberally with pesto (about 1 Tbs.).
4. Top with pieces of julienned ham and garnish with a small basil leaf.

My Way:
Julienne is a French technique of cutting meats or vegetables into similar-size rectangular pieces, roughly the size of a matchstick or larger.

"Create a visual feast as well as an edible one."
— D.J.

Red Pepper Salad with Sun Dried Tomatoes and Olives

Serves 6.

12	large leaves of red lettuce, washed, dried, and crisped
3	large red peppers, roasted, peeled, and cut into strips
10	sun-dried tomato halves, drained of oil and sliced into thirds
4	ripe Roma tomatoes
4 Tbs.	extra-virgin olive oil
2 tsp.	fresh lemon juice
	Salt and freshly ground black pepper to taste
1 tsp.	marjoram
2 oz.	black Kalamata or Italian olives marinated in oil and herbs

1. Prepare the lettuce and chill.
2. Roast, peel, and slice the peppers. Place in a bowl and set aside.
3. Blanch the fresh Roma tomatoes in boiling water for 30 seconds and peel off the skin. Slice tomatoes, discarding most of the seeds, and mix them with the prepared slices of sun-dried tomatoes.
4. Add tomatoes to the red pepper slices and toss. Add the marjoram, salt, pepper, and olives; toss again.
5. Place olive oil, lemon juice, salt, and pepper in a jar, and shake well. Add to the vegetables and toss them again.
6. Place lettuce leaves on salad plates and top with the dressed vegetable mixture. Serve along with crusty Italian bread and butter, or little bowls of extra-virgin olive oil for dipping the bread.

My Way:

Roasting Peppers: This is the easiest way I have found to roast and skin peppers: Cut each pepper in half, discarding core and seeds, and trim away any white parts. Place, skin side up, on a cookie sheet sprayed with oil. Smash peppers down as flat as possible. Broil on high 3 to 4 inches from heat until skins are totally blackened. Seal in a plastic bag and leave for 5 to 10 minutes to steam and cool. Carefully remove peppers from the bag and peel with your fingers under cold, running water.

You may freeze roasted, peeled peppers for future use, or cover them with olive or canola oil and store in the refrigerator for up to one week. They're great with hors d'oeuvres, in soups, with pasta or risotto, and cooked in a myriad of other things, like omelets, etc. Be creative!

Curried Risotto Venezia
with Shrimp and Asparagus

I love risotto because it is delicious and easy to prepare, and an infinite combination of ingredients marry well with the dish. This risotto was served to me on my birthday in Venice, at a restaurant that had once been a beautiful Venetian villa. The addition of the curry made the risotto quite different than any I'd ever tasted.

This recipe without the shrimp, asparagus, and curry is a basic risotto. You can add whatever you like instead of these ingredients or simply serve as is, as a rice dish. Arborio rice cooks differently than regular long-grain rice and has a delicious, nutty flavor. Risotto is best made just before serving.

Serves 6.

1-1/2 lbs.	large, raw shrimp in the shell
	Olive oil, for sautéing
1-1/2 lbs.	fresh asparagus
1/2 c.	grated Parmesan cheese
3 Tbs.	butter
1 Tbs.	curry powder (Make sure it's fresh; buy in bulk!)
1/2 c.	minced onion
2 c.	arborio rice
5 c.	chicken stock, heated
1/2 c.	dry white wine
1 tsp.	salt
	Freshly ground black pepper to taste
1/2 c.	grated Parmesan cheese, for garnish
1/2 c.	minced fresh Italian parsley

1. Shell and devein the shrimp, and rinse in cold water. Set aside.

2. Heat 2 Tbs. olive oil in a sauté pan on medium-high heat. Add the shrimp, salt lightly, and sauté until the shrimp is pink in color and just cooked through, about 4 to 5 minutes. Set aside.

3. Clean the asparagus, break off and discard the ends, and steam in a vegetable steamer until it is crisp-tender and still bright green in color, 3 to 4 minutes. Rinse quickly in cold water to stop the cooking. When cool enough to

My Way:

A rubber spatula works best for stirring cooked foods. It is gentler on the food and doesn't break it up at all, like metal does.

handle, cut into thirds, and set aside.

4. Grate cheese and set aside.

5. Begin the risotto: Melt 3 Tbs. butter in a heavy saucepan. Add the curry powder and cook lightly 2 to 3 minutes. (This mellows the sharp flavor that curry has before cooking.)

6. Add the minced onion and sauté 2 to 3 minutes over low heat. Do not brown.

7. Add the rice and stir to coat with the curry mixture. Pour in the white wine and cook on low heat until the wine is absorbed. Do not cover the pan. Stir occasionally with *rubber* spatula to prevent sticking (see "My Way.") Watch carefully.

8. Heat the chicken stock. Add 1/2 c. stock to the rice, and cook until it is absorbed, stirring occasionally. It should be simmering slightly, with little movement in the liquid.

9. Continue to add the stock in half-cup increments till the rice is tender but still slightly crunchy in the center, about 30 minutes. Do not cover the pan at any time. You may or may not need all of the stock. (Store any leftover stock in the refrigerator for another use.)

10. Add salt and pepper to taste, plus the remaining 3 Tbs. butter, and fold in gently with a rubber spatula.

11. Fold in the shrimp, asparagus, and 1/2 c. of the cheese, and stir gently. Garnish with minced parsley and serve immediately, passing the remaining 1/2 c. of cheese at the table.

Zuccotto with Raspberry Sauce

Delicious! And easier to prepare by using store-bought pound cake. Make batches of Raspberry Sauce when the fruit is in season, and freeze it for dessert toppings throughout the year.

Serves 10 to 12.

2 oz.	blanched almonds, coarsely chopped
2 oz.	shelled hazelnuts (filberts)
1 (12-oz.)	pound cake, frozen (Sara Lee brand works best)
3 Tbs.	cognac, or other good-quality brandy
2 Tbs.	maraschino cherry liqueur
2 Tbs.	Cointreau
5 oz.	semisweet chocolate, coarsely chopped
1/2 c.	chopped maraschino cherries
2 c.	heavy cream, cold
3/4 c.	powdered sugar

Raspberry Sauce:

1 pt.	fresh raspberries
1 Tbs.	granulated sugar
1 Tbs.	Kirsch liqueur
	Pinch of salt

1. Preheat oven to 325 degrees. Place hazelnuts on a baking sheet and bake for about 5 minutes to dry skins. Remove nuts from oven and chop coarsely; set aside along with the chopped almonds.
2. Line a 1-1/2 — quart mold (a rounded mixing bowl works very well) with a layer of damp cheesecloth large enough to hang over the edge of the mold and cover the top. (Cheesecloth can be found in most supermarkets or gourmet kitchen shops.)
3. Cut pound cake in slices 3/8-inch thick. Then cut each slice on the diagonal, making two triangular sections.
4. Mix together the brandy, maraschino liqueur, and the Cointreau in a small bowl. Moisten each cake triangle with a sprinkling of the liqueurs and place it firmly against the inside of the cheesecloth-lined mold, narrowest end at the bottom, till the inside of the bowl is completely lined with moistened sections of cake. Push together to fill in all the gaps. Set aside any extra cake slices.

5. In another bowl whip the cold, heavy cream and gradually add the powdered sugar, whipping till stiff. Mix in the chopped almonds, hazelnuts, cherries, and 3 oz. of the chocolate pieces. Divide the mixture into two equal parts. Set aside half and spoon the other half into the cake-lined bowl, spreading evenly over the whole surface.

6. Gently heat remaining 2 oz. of chocolate in a small pan or in the microwave just until melted. Fold the melted chocolate into remaining half of the whipped-cream mixture. Spoon this into the cake bowl until the cavity is completely filled. Even off the top of the bowl with a knife, cutting off any protruding pieces of cake.

7. Lay any remaining pound cake slices, moistened with the liqueurs, on top of the dessert. Trim edges so that it rests completely flat in the mold. Cover with the overlapped cheese cloth and then some plastic wrap, and refrigerate overnight, or up to 2 days.

8. Make the raspberry sauce: Purée fruit, sugar, Kirsch liqueur, and salt in a food processor. Strain half or all of the seeds out of the sauce in a fine sieve. Chill until ready to use.

9. When ready to serve, remove the molded dessert from the refrigerator. Take off the plastic wrap and peel back the cheesecloth. Place a flat serving tray with low sides over the top and invert the zuccotto. Lift off the bowl and carefully peel off the cheesecloth. Serve cold in wedges with fresh raspberry sauce, drizzling some of the sauce over the whole zuccotto and passing the rest separately.

Italian Menu #2:

A Romantic Summer Dinner in Italy

Bruschetta Romano Crostini
Tomato Basil Soup
Tossed Greens with Fresh Mozzerella and Pine Nuts
Chicken Piccata
Ziti in Broccoli Sauce
Zabaglione alla Frutta

How blessed we are to reap the harvest of richness and abundance of summer fruits and vegetables, reflected in this meal. Nature's harvest begins with a variety of greens from lettuces to beans and broccoli. As summer progresses, so do tomatoes, and this soup is delicious made with fresh, vine-ripened, succulent tomatoes. The fruits in the dessert are plentiful and ripe, ensuring fresh, intense flavors. This menu offers a variety of taste sensations and textures. Simple, yet satisfying — truly, food for the soul!

Bruschetta Romano Crostini

Serves 4 to 6.

3/4 tsp.	red wine vinegar
1/2 c.	extra-virgin olive oil
6 Tbs.	minced fresh Italian parsley
3 Tbs.	minced fresh basil
1 small can	anchovies, minced
1	large clove garlic, crushed
1/4 tsp.	red pepper flakes
1	medium tomato, chopped, seeded, and juice removed
2 Tbs.	chopped green pepper
8 slices	baguette bread, sliced about 1/2-inch thick
1 Tbs.	extra-virgin olive

1. Whisk together the vinegar and oil, and then stir in the parsley and basil.
2. Place anchovies, garlic, and red pepper flakes in food processor and process until smooth.
3. Slowly add the oil-and-vinegar mixture and let sit for 2 hours to meld flavors. Then add the chopped tomatoes and chopped green pepper, and stir.
4. Grill or toast the bread slices (on barbecue or in oven) until crisp and hot. While warm, brush with olive oil. Spread with anchovy mixture and serve immediately with red wine.

"Italians portray their sensuality in their food. Sensuality and food are closely connected — another reason why people love cooking with Spirit!"

— D.J.

Tomato Basil Soup

Serves 6 to 8.

8 Tbs.	butter
2	large yellow onions, sliced (about 2 c.)
4	cloves garlic, peeled and minced
1 tsp.	curry powder
8 c. (2 qts.)	chicken stock
8 c.	fresh chopped tomatoes, peeled and seeded, or 2 (35-oz.) cans Italian plum tomatoes, drained (reserve liquid for another use) Salt and freshly ground black pepper to taste Pinch sugar
1 bunch	fresh basil, leaves only, finely chopped
3	fresh Roma tomatoes, cored, seeded, and cut in 1/2-inch dice

Whole, fresh basil leaves, for garnish
Sour cream

1. In a large stockpot, melt butter over low heat.
2. Add onion and garlic. Cook, covered, over low heat 20 minutes, stirring occasionally. Add the curry powder in the last 5 minutes and continue to cook.
3. Add chicken stock, drained tomatoes, salt, pepper, sugar, and half of the chopped basil. Stir well and bring to a boil.
4. Reduce heat and simmer, covered, over low heat for 45 minutes.
5. Remove from heat and cool slightly. In small batches, purée the soup in a blender.
6. Return soup to pot. Add remaining chopped basil; simmer 5 minutes. Add the diced, fresh tomatoes.
7. Garnish with a dollop of sour cream and a fresh basil leaf.

My Way:
In ALL ingredients I always feel that FRESH IS BEST. Of course, that's not always possible, so be flexible and use what you can and what you have. And don't be afraid to experiment! That's the best way to learn and come up with new concoctions.

Tossed Greens with Fresh Mozzarella and Pine Nuts

Serves 4 to 6.

1	fresh buffalo mozzarella cheese (packed in water, about 7 oz.; found in the deli section)
1	ripe avocado, stoned, peeled, and sliced
1/2 c.	coarsely chopped roasted red peppers
12	pitted black Italian olives
12	pimento-stuffed green olives
5 Tbs.	extra-virgin olive oil
	Freshly ground black pepper
1/2 c.	pine nuts
1/4 c.	minced fresh Italian parsley

1. Slice the cheese thinly and arrange the pieces in a circle on a round platter.
2. Top each cheese slice with a slice of avocado and a slice of red pepper. Scatter the olives all around.
3. Sprinkle the olive oil over all, top with freshly ground pepper and salt lightly.
4. Toast the pine nuts in a dry pan on top of the stove until golden brown. Cool, and sprinkle over the salad along with the minced parsley.

"Don't get prayer and God and Spirit confused with religion. They can be entirely different things."

— D.J.

Chicken Piccata

An easy-to-prepare dish with great flavor and very tender chicken — if you don't overcook it!

Serves 6 to 8.

1-1/2 lbs.	boned and skinned chicken breasts, pounded thin and cut into 3-inch pieces
3/4 c.	flour
1/2 tsp.	salt
1/4 tsp.	white pepper
4 Tbs.	butter
4 Tbs.	extra-virgin olive oil
1/2 c.	chicken stock
1 c.	dry white wine
1/2 tsp.	salt
	Freshly ground black pepper
2 Tbs.	capers, rinsed and drained
1	lemon, sliced thin
1 Tbs.	minced fresh Italian parsley

1. Prepare chicken breasts.
2. Place flour, salt, and white pepper in a flat plate and mix well. Dip each piece of the chicken in the flour and place on another plate.
3. Heat 1 Tbs. butter and 1 Tbs. olive oil in a heavy skillet over medium heat until the butter and oil are bubbling.
4. Sauté the chicken quickly, a few pieces at a time, using about 1 Tbs. of oil and butter each time. This should only take 3 to 4 minutes a side. Do not overcook. Remove the chicken when golden brown to a warm platter. Keep covered.
5. Pour the chicken stock into the pan drippings. Simmer gently, stirring up the brown bits with a wooden spoon. Add the wine and salt and simmer 1 minute.
6. Return chicken to the skillet and cook, covered, 2 to 3 minutes till simmering gently and heated through. The sauce should reduce to about half and thicken slightly.
7. Season with freshly ground black pepper and add the capers. Stir with a rubber spatula. To serve, arrange the chicken on a large platter. Pour the caper sauce over the chicken and garnish with the lemon slices and minced parsley.

"Cooking with Spirit is an act of love."
— D.J.

Ziti in Broccoli Sauce

Even people who don't like broccoli love this sauce!

Serves 6 to 8.

8 cloves	garlic
1/4 c.	canola oil
1/4 c.	extra-virgin olive oil, plus more as needed
1	large bunch broccoli
1 lb.	ziti pasta, or your choice of tubular pasta
1/2 c.	grated Parmesan or Romano cheese, optional

1. Preheat oven to 400 degrees. Peel the garlic cloves and place in a small, oven-proof dish. Blend the two oils and add enough to the dish to cover the garlic. Bake till brown, about 15 to 20 minutes. Remove from oven and cool.
2. Trim the broccoli and steam till just tender, but still nice and bright green.
3. Drain, cool, and cut into chunks that will fit into the food processor.
4. Place in food processor and turn on and off to chop the broccoli.
5. Add the cooked garlic and then its cooking oil in a steady stream to the broccoli. Process till the mixture is of a thick, saucelike consistency. Add extra olive oil if needed. Season with salt and pepper.
6. Boil the ziti in salted water until al dente, about 10 minutes. Test by tasting one.
7. Toss the ziti well with the broccoli sauce and serve immediately with grated Parmesan or Romano cheese if you wish.

Zabaglione alla Frutta

This dessert is so easy to make, yet tastes complex and delicious. You may use almost any variety of fruit. Leave thin-skinned fruits such as apples, pears, and nectarines unpeeled; do peel bananas, oranges, grapefruits, or other fruits with inedible skins.

Serves 6.

1	apple, cored, and sliced
1	pear, cored, and sliced
1	nectarine, cored, and sliced
2	bananas, peeled and sliced thick
2 Tbs.	fresh lemon juice
8	large egg yolks
2/3 c.	granulated sugar
4 oz.	Marsala wine
4 oz.	dry white wine
4 Tbs.	powdered sugar
1 c.	fresh raspberries

"I give thanks in advance for all my good."
— Anonymous

1. Dip cut fruit, (not the berries) into the lemon juice to prevent browning, and arrange in a flame-proof dish.
2. Beat the egg yolks with the sugar until pale, then add the Marsala and white wine.
3. Place the bowl over a pan of barely simmering water, and continue whisking until mixture starts swelling to a thick foam and sticks to the base of the bowl. Stir constantly but gently.
4. Pour mixture over the fruit and sprinkle the surface with the raspberries and powdered sugar.
5. Place briefly under a preheated broiler, and grill until the sugar begins to brown and caramelize. You need nothing else with this dessert.

Italian Menu #3:

An Italian Dinner alla Milanese

Artichoke Hearts Gorgonzola on Rustic Baguette
Roasted Red Pepper Soup Sambuca
Lobster Risotto
Macaroon Stuffed Peaches in Madeira Wine

This is a very elegant Italian dinner that everyone loves. You can prepare a lot of it ahead, everything except the risotto. Serve with your favorite bread and wine. Before partaking of this meal, begin with a short meditation acknowledging Mother Earth for her gifts from land and sea. Focus on the abundance you are about to receive. Give thanks, and then enjoy the flavors of full-bodied gorgonzola cheese, roasted peppers in chicken stock, and rich, sweet, lobster risotto.

Artichokes Hearts Gorgonzola
on Rustic Baguette

Serves 6 to 8.

2 small jars	marinated artichoke hearts, drained
8 Tbs.	extra-virgin olive oil
3 Tbs.	fresh lemon juice
1	clove garlic, minced
2 Tbs.	grated Parmesan cheese
	Freshly ground black pepper to taste
3 oz.	gorgonzola cheese, crumbled
	Cherry tomatoes

1. Finely chop the artichoke hearts.
2. Mix together olive oil, lemon juice, minced garlic, Parmesan cheese, and black pepper to taste; pour over artichokes, toss, and marinate overnight.
3. To serve, place in a serving bowl and sprinkle the crumbled gorgonzola cheese over the mixture. Garnish the bowl with cherry tomatoes around the edges. Serve as an appetizer with Italian rustic baguette.

"Of all the knowledge, the wise seek most to know themselves."
— William Shakespeare

Roasted Red Pepper Soup Sambuca

Sometimes I serve little liqueur glasses half-filled with Sambuca on the side to sip slowly after each mouthful of soup, or pour 1 Tbs. in individual brandy snifters set at each person's soup bowl. Flame the Sambuca, and let each guest pour it into their soup.

Serves 6.

4 Tbs.	butter
3	large onions, sliced
2	cloves garlic, minced
1 tsp.	salt
4 c.	roasted red peppers
3 to 4 c.	chicken stock
1/2 c.	heavy cream
	Salt and freshly ground black pepper to taste
1/4 tsp.	ground cayenne pepper
3 Tbs.	Sambuca liqueur

Chopped fresh Italian parsley

1. Melt butter in a large, heavy saucepan over medium heat. Add onions, garlic, and salt, and sauté for about 10 minutes or until tender.
2. Add the peppers and chicken stock to the onions, and simmer for 15 minutes.
3. Purée mixture in food processor or blender until smooth. Transfer purée to a saucepan, and bring to a simmer.
4. Stir in cream, and season with salt, pepper, and cayenne. Thin with additional chicken stock if necessary.
5. Add the Sambuca liqueur, stir, and serve immediately, garnished with chopped Italian parsley. Do not add the liqueur until just ready to serve.

Live in the present.
Learn from the past.
Look forward to the
future with anticipation and
a positive attitude.

D.J.

Lobster Risotto

LOBSTER RISOTTO

This risotto is melt-in-your-mouth delicious. Serve small portions to start, as it is rich.

Serves 6 to 8.

7 c.	fresh chicken stock
4 Tbs.	butter
1/3 c.	finely chopped onion
2 c.	arborio rice
1/2 c.	dry white wine
1/8 tsp.	saffron
4 Tbs.	butter, softened
1 lb.	cooked lobster meat, cut in bite-size chunks
2	ripe tomatoes, blanched, peeled, chopped, and drained of juice and seeds
1/4 c.	minced fresh Italian parsley

1. Bring chicken stock to a simmer over low heat.
2. In a heavy 3-quart saucepan, melt the butter over moderate heat.
3. Add chopped onions and cook 7 to 8 minutes, stirring frequently. Do not brown.
4. Add rice and stir with a spatula till rice is coated with butter, about 1 to 2 minutes.
5. Pour in the wine and simmer until liquid is almost completely absorbed.
6. Add about 1-1/2 c. hot chicken stock to the rice and cook, uncovered, stirring occasionally until stock is almost absorbed.
7. Stir the saffron into another 1-1/2 c. of hot stock and add it to the rice. Simmer again until almost absorbed.
8. Add remaining stock, 1/2 c. at a time, just until the rice is cooked but is still slightly crunchy in the center. Taste it and add more salt if necessary.
9. Add the lobster and tomatoes, and stir gently with a rubber spatula to heat through.
10. Add the Parmesan cheese and stir. The rice should be very moist; you may need to add a little more stock or wine if it is too dry. Serve immediately, garnished with minced Italian parsley.

"Slow down. There's nothing more precious than NOW."

— *Inneractions,*
Paul and Collins

"I pray for the earth to become the planet of peace."
— Anonymous

Loneliness is the most terrible poverty.
Mother Theresa

Macroon Stuffed Peaches in Madeira Wine

Serves 8.

16	canned peach halves, drained
	Fresh lemon juice
1/3 c.	peach pulp, scooped out of centers of above peach halves
3/4 c.	macaroon crumbs
1/3 c.	finely chopped toasted almonds
5 Tbs.	sugar
1/3 c.	Madeira wine
1 c.	heavy cream
2 Tbs.	powdered sugar
1 tsp.	vanilla extract
1/4 c.	slivered almonds, toasted, for garnish

1. Preheat oven to 350 degrees. Place drained peach halves on paper towel to absorb excess liquid; then place 8 of them, cut side up, in an oven-proof dish. Remove a bit of pulp from the peach centers to make room for filling, and reserve 1/3 c. of the pulp.
2. In a small bowl, mix macaroon crumbs with 1/3 c. toasted almonds, 2 Tbs. sugar, and 1/3 c. reserved peach pulp.
3. Spoon 1 Tbs. filling into each of the 8 peach halves.
4. Place remaining halves on top to resemble whole peaches and secure with toothpicks.
5. Return to baking dish and brush liberally with lemon juice.
6. Sprinkle remaining 3 Tbs. sugar over the peaches and pour Madeira around them. Cover and bake for 15 minutes.
7. Cool uncovered, then chill. Remove toothpicks before serving.
8. Whip the cream, slowly adding the powdered sugar and vanilla until soft peaks form. Serve peaches in stemmed glasses, topped with whipped cream and a few extra toasted almonds.

Italian Menu #4:

On the Italian Riviera

Grilled Vegetables Bagna Cauda
Tossed Vegetable Salad with Anchovy Dressing
Linguine with Scallops Marinara
Gnocchi Verde
Black and White Souffle, Peasant Style
Vanilla Custard

The cruise ships come and go here in Positano, on the Italian Riviera. Tourists come ashore to explore this charming town built up on high, seaside cliffs. I spent ten days here one summer at a charming hotel, high up among the winding streets. We visited some of the excellent restaurants along our walks down to the beach. Each time we passed through the steep, narrow streets, the locals and shop owners greeted us with "Buon giorno!" What charming, friendly people! I felt very much at home, like one of the locals. It seemed like a lifetime spent there. It was difficult to leave this wonderful village.

Grilled Vegetables Bagna Cauda

A classic Italian first course. I know many of you will be saying, "Yuck, I hate anchovies," but trust me, this is delicious! It is a great combination with any grilled vegetables, or even fresh, uncooked ones. Always rinse anchovies in a sieve under cool running water to remove some of their sharp taste. Blending with the other ingredients also smoothes out that fish taste. This is about as Italian for a first course as you can get.

Serves 6 to 8.

Bagna Cauda:

6	cloves garlic, peeled
9 oz.	anchovy fillets, packed in oil, drained, and rinsed
	Juice and finely chopped zest of 2 lemons
2 c.	extra-virgin olive oil
	Freshly ground black pepper to taste

Vegetables:

4	fennel bulbs, tough outer leaves removed and bulb cut into quarters (using white part only)
2 to 3	radicchio hearts, cut into quarters
2 lbs.	green beans, blanched
20	small red potatoes, scrubbed and cooked until tender
1-1/2 c.	fresh mushrooms
2 lbs.	baby carrots, peeled with stalks left on and blanched
	Extra-virgin olive oil
	Salt
1	fresh hot, red chile, seeds removed and minced fine, optional

1. To make the bagna cauda, pound the garlic to a paste with a mortar and pestle or whirl in the food processor if you must. Add the anchovies and combine until the mixture forms a paste.

2. Transfer paste to a small saucepan, add lemon juice and zest, then stir in gradually 2 c. of olive oil. Season with some freshly ground black pepper and place over low heat. Do not allow to boil, just heat through to combine and soften the flavors.

"If time is running away with you, your life is not in order."
— The Peace Pilgrim

3. Cook vegetables by tossing them in some olive oil and salt, then grilling on a flat pan either on top of the stove or on a grill or barbecue, until cooked and browned a bit.

4. To serve, place warm bagna cauda in a small bowl and stir in the fresh minced chile. Serve on a platter, surrounded with vegetables for dipping.

Tossed Vegetable Salad with Anchovy Dressing

Serves 6 to 8.

Dressing:

2	anchovies, finely minced, or 1 Tbs. anchovy paste
1 clove	garlic, minced
2 Tbs.	red wine vinegar
1 tsp.	Dijon mustard
6 Tbs.	extra-virgin olive oil
	Freshly ground black pepper to taste
1 Tbs.	capers, drained, rinsed, and minced

Salad:

1	large head romaine lettuce, washed, drained, and torn into bite-size pieces
1	small red onion, sliced thin
2	ripe tomatoes, washed and cut into bite-size pieces
1/2	green pepper, cut into julienne strips
1/2	cucumber, sliced
1	stalk celery, washed and sliced
1/2 c.	marinated artichoke hearts, drained
3 Tbs.	grated Parmesan cheese
1 c.	garlic croutons, homemade or packaged

1. Place all dressing ingredients in a jar and shake well. If using whole anchovies, be sure to rinse them well and drain before mincing.
2. Place all salad ingredients except cheese and croutons into a large salad bowl.
3. Add dressing and toss. Add cheese and croutons, and toss again. Serve immediately.

I am whole and healthy in mind, body and spirit.
Daily Word

Linguine with Scallops Marinara

You won't need to take your daily garlic pills with this meal. Just remember garlic is VERY good for you in helping to prevent disease. Remember, when making tomato-based sauces such as marinara, it's best to use only wooden spoons for stirring, as contact with metal changes the flavor of the tomatoes, making them more acidic.

Serves 6.

Marinara Sauce:

2 Tbs.	extra-virgin olive oil
2 cloves	garlic, peeled and cut in half
5 to 6 sprigs	fresh basil
2 to 3 sprigs	fresh Italian parsley
1 large can	Italian plum tomatoes
	Dry white wine

Linguine:

1 lb.	large sea scallops
8 Tbs.	extra-virgin olive oil
1 Tbs.	finely chopped garlic
2 Tbs.	minced garlic
2 Tbs.	minced fresh Italian parsley
	Salt to taste
1/4 tsp.	red pepper flakes
1 lb.	linguine noodles
1/4 c.	bread crumbs, lightly toasted in a frying pan with a little olive oil, as garnish
	Minced fresh Italian parsley, for garnish

1. Make the sauce: In a large sauté pan, heat the oil and add the four garlic halves. Sauté on medium heat until the garlic is golden brown. Discard the garlic.
2. Take the pan off the heat and carefully add the can of plum tomatoes, watching so that you don't get spattered with hot oil. Break the tomatoes down with a wooden spoon and put back on the heat.
3. Add the basil and parsley, and simmer very gently on low heat until the liquid is reduced and you have a nice, thick sauce of medium consistency, about 20 minutes. If it gets too thick, add a little white wine to thin it down. Remove the basil and parsley sprigs. At this point you

Life is like playing a violin solo in public and learning the instrument as one goes along.

Samuel Butler

may reserve the sauce until everything else is ready and then reheat, or make ahead and refrigerate for up to 2 days.

4. For the linguine, wash scallops thoroughly in cold water and pat dry. Slice them in half vertically to resemble small, thin scallops.

5. Heat the oil in a sauté pan and add the garlic. Cook briefly until golden. Add the parsley and the red pepper flakes.

6. Stir once or twice, then add the scallops and 2 large pinches of salt.

7. Turn the heat to high and cook for about 1-1/2 minutes, stirring frequently, until the scallops lose their shine and turn a flat white. Do not overcook the scallops or they will become tough. If scallops shed a lot of liquid, remove them from the pan with a slotted spoon and boil down the watery juices. Return scallops to the pan, turn them quickly, then remove from heat.

8. Taste for seasoning and correct, adding more salt and red pepper flakes if necessary.

9. Cook the pasta al dente in boiling water with 2 Tbs. olive oil and 2 tsp. salt. Drain pasta and toss with 1 Tbs. olive oil.

10. Place the linguine on a platter or on individual plates, then top with marinara sauce and some of the scallops. Sprinkle with the toasted bread crumbs and fresh parsley, and serve immediately.

Gnocci Verde

Gnocci are delicious and a unique way to present spinach. I have made them many times and find that using frozen spinach doesn't affect the quality of the flavors. Frozen spinach also saves time, as it takes a while to wash and dry that much fresh spinach.

Serves 8.

4 Tbs.	butter
2 pkgs.	frozen, chopped spinach, defrosted, squeezed completely dry, and chopped fine; or 1-1/2 lbs. fresh spinach, washed and steamed until limp(10-oz. pkg.)
3/4 c.	ricotta cheese
2	large eggs, lightly beaten
6 Tbs.	flour
3/4 c.	grated Parmesan cheese
1/2 tsp.	salt
1/2 tsp.	freshly ground black pepper
Large pinch	ground nutmeg, preferably fresh
6 to 8 qts.	water
1 Tbs.	salt
4 Tbs.	melted butter

1. Heat 4 Tbs. butter in skillet over medium heat until melted.
2. Add chopped spinach and cook, stirring constantly, 2 to 3 minutes till all moisture has evaporated.
3. Add 3/4 c. ricotta cheese and cook, stirring, 3 to 4 minutes.
4. Transfer ingredients to a large bowl and mix in the lightly beaten eggs, flour, 1/4 c. of the grated Parmesan cheese, salt, pepper, and nutmeg.
5. Place in refrigerator for 30 to 60 minutes, or till firm.
6. Put water and salt in a large pot and bring to a simmer over moderate heat. Meanwhile, flour your hands lightly and mold spinach mixture into 1-1/2 -inch gnocchi balls. You may chill the gnocchi for 30 to 60 minutes at this point or cook right away.
7. Gently drop balls into just simmering water and cook, uncovered, 5 to 8 minutes or until they puff up and float to the top of the water. If the water is simmering too

hard, the gnocci will fall apart. Remove gnocchi to paper towels to drain.

8. Pour 2 Tbs. melted butter into an 8x12-inch gratin dish. Arrange the drained gnocci in the dish in one layer.

9. Dribble the remaining 2 Tbs. melted butter over them and sprinkle with the remaining 1/2 c. grated Parmesan cheese.

10. Place in preheated broiler 3 inches away from heat for 3 minutes, or until cheese melts. Serve at once.

Black and White Soufflé, Peasant Style

I had the pleasure of tasting this soufflé at a wonderful hotel in Ravello. The area there is very hilly and covered for miles with vineyards. We were seated at an outdoor patio hanging over a high hillside cliff with a spectacular 90-degree view. We ate a leisurely, two-plus — hour lunch, Italian style, ordering as we went along and ending with this wonderful dessert. It was a memorable lunch, never to be forgotten. Of course, I got out my notepad and made copious notes throughout so I wouldn't forget anything by the time I reached my own kitchen at home.

Serves 8.

2 Tbs.	orange zest
6 Tbs.	sugar
8	large eggs, separated while cold (the yolk has less chance of breaking that way. Be sure not to mix any of the yolk with the whites or they will not beat up stiff.)
3 oz.	semisweet chocolate (three 1-oz. squares)
2 Tbs.	milk
4 Tbs.	cornstarch
2/3 c.	sugar
1/4 tsp.	salt
2/3 c.	milk
4 Tbs.	orange liqueur
1/4 tsp.	cream of tartar
4 Tbs.	powdered sugar

My Way:
In very small amounts, salt adds flavor even to sweet dishes. It also prevents sweets from tasting flat.

1. Mix the orange zest and 6 Tbs. sugar together and store in the refrigerator overnight to let flavor intensify.
2. Preheat oven to 350 degrees. Butter a large oval or rectangular oven-proof dish, and sprinkle the sides and bottom of the dish with the sugar and orange zest mixture.
3. Separate eggs. Place whites in a large mixing bowl and set aside to warm to room temperature (you'll get more volume from them this way.) Place yolks in another bowl, beat them well, and set aside.
4. Melt chocolate in 2 Tbs. milk in microwave oven.
5. Combine the cornstarch, 2/3 c. sugar, and salt in a saucepan. Add the milk and stir till smooth. Cook over

medium heat, stirring constantly till mixture thickens and bubbles gently. Remove from heat.

6. Beat mixture slowly into the egg yolks, stirring gently with a rubber spatula, and then cool.

7. Pour half of this mixture into another bowl and add the chocolate mixture and the orange liqueur to it, stirring well. Set aside both the "white" and "black" bowls of soufflé mixture.

8. Add cream of tartar to the egg whites. Beat until whites form stiff peaks when beater is lifted out slowly, but do not overbeat.

9. Pile half the egg whites into the chocolate mixture, and the remaining egg whites into the white custard mixture. Fold the whites into each mixture with a rubber spatula.

10. Transfer the white soufflé to one side of the prepared baking dish and the chocolate mixture onto the other side of the dish. They will blend together in the center in a marbleized pattern. Sprinkle with the powdered sugar.

11. Bake 45 to 50 minutes, or until soufflé is puffed and fairly firm to the touch but not dry. Serve immediately with Vanilla Custard on the side.

Vanilla Custard

Serves 8.

4	large egg yolks
1/2 c.	sugar
1-3/4 c.	milk
1 to 2 tsp.	vanilla extract

1. Beat egg yolks and sugar till thick.
2. Bring milk to a boil and gradually pour into the egg yolk/sugar mixture, whisking all the while.
3. Pour mixture into a heavy saucepan and cook, stirring constantly, till custard coats a wooden spoon with a light film. Do not boil.
4. Strain custard, add vanilla, and chill.

*

"True joy comes from the deep feeling of being alive with Spirit."

— D.J.

Italian Menu #5:

Dinner in Rome with Armando

Baked Zucchini and Parmesan
Grilled Bread with Pesto and Beef Slices
Mozzarella Tomato Salad
Lemon-Scented Salmon Fettuccini
Gelati and Pecan Praline Sauce

God bless Armando! He taught me how to eat pasta the way the Romans do, with a spoon used as a support to wind the pasta around the dinner fork. It took me at least 30 minutes to eat this pasta, but by that time, I was adept at eating pasta properly. Armando was a wonderful guide who taught us a great deal about native Romans and especially about restaurants and food. He knew them all, and loved his Italian food. He would love this meal, too.

Baked Zucchini and Parmesan

Serves 8 to 16.

8	medium zucchini
1/2 c.	finely grated Parmesan cheese, plus extra for topping
1 to 2 Tbs.	minced fresh basil
2 Tbs.	chopped red onion
1	clove garlic, minced
	Salt and freshly ground black pepper to taste

1. Preheat oven to 400 degrees. Cook whole zucchini in boiling, salted water just until al dente.
2. Drain and cut the zucchini in half lengthwise.
3. Mix the Parmesan, basil, onion, and garlic together well.
4. Sprinkle the cheese mixture over the zucchini halves and place on a flat cookie sheet or baking dish. Sprinkle with salt and pepper.
5. Top with a little more cheese and bake for 15 minutes or until the top is golden.

"Follow your heart."
— Anonymous

Grilled Bread with Pesto and Beef Slices

The leftovers from Barbecued Flank Steak are perfect to use for this appetizer, or cook a fresh steak and save the rest for another meal.

Serves 4 to 6; may double or triple.

Pesto:

2 c.	loosely packed fresh basil leaves
1/2 c.	extra-virgin olive oil
2	large cloves garlic
1 tsp.	salt
	Freshly ground black pepper to taste
1 Tbs.	pine nuts or walnuts

Bread and Beef:

12 slices	good baguette bread or other dense French or Italian bread
2 to 3 oz.	Barbecued Flank Steak, thinly sliced

1. Make the pesto: In food processor place basil, olive oil, garlic, salt, pepper, and pine nuts. Process until a saucelike mixture forms. You may need to add more oil. Set aside.
2. Grill the bread in a lightly oiled frying pan until golden, or toast dry on a cookie sheet in a 350-degree oven for 10 to15 minutes.
3. Spread each piece of bread liberally with pesto, about 1 Tbs.
4. Top with pieces of Barbecued Flank Steak and garnish with a small basil leaf.

Mozzarella Tomato Salad

This salad is also great to take on a picnic. All you need to go with it are some good bread, fruit, and Italian wine, and you're set for a memorable and easy-on-your-time feast.

Serves 6 to 8.

	Lettuce leaves
1 lb.	fresh buffalo mozzarella cheese (packed in water), drained and sliced thin
1 lb.	fresh, ripe tomatoes, sliced thin
1 bunch	fresh basil, washed and dried
1/2 c.	Italian olives
	Salt and freshly ground black pepper to taste
4 Tbs.	extra-virgin olive oil

1. Wash and dry the lettuce leaves, and line a serving dish with them.
2. Arrange the cheese and the tomatoes alternately over the lettuce leaves along with the basil leaves, and scatter the olives over the whole salad.
3. Add salt and pepper, and drizzle the olive oil over all. Serve with good Italian bread and the wine of your choice, red or white.

"Dear Spirit, what can I do to create an atmosphere of peace?"

— D.J.

Lemon Scented Salmon Fettuccine

This sauce is great with any variety of foods from chicken to shrimp to vegetables in season. It has far less calories than the standard fettuccine sauce. It is very healthy and flavorful, and you won't miss all that cream at all!

Serves 4.

2 c.	chicken stock
1/2	medium-sized fennel bulb, finely chopped, feathery leaf top reserved
1	medium onion, finely chopped
1/2 c.	heavy cream
	Salt and freshly ground black pepper
1 lb.	fettuccine noodles, fresh or dried
2	lemons, zest and juice, or to taste
3/4 lb.	smoked salmon, julienned

1. Place chicken stock, chopped fennel bulb, and onion in a saucepan. Cook over medium heat until fennel is very tender, about 10 minutes.
2. Add heavy cream and bring the mixture to a boil. Remove pan from heat and pour contents into a blender.
3. Purée and season to taste with a little salt and pepper (remember that the salmon will add salt too.) Pour the purée into a large skillet and set aside.
4. Cook fettuccine in a large pot of salted boiling water until al dente, about 3 to 4 minutes for fresh, and about 8 to 10 minutes for dried. Drain.
5. While the pasta is cooking, bring fennel purée to a simmer. Reduce heat to low and add fettuccine, lemon zest and juice, and smoked salmon. Toss well. Taste for seasoning.
6. Toss mixture again and heat through for about 30 seconds. Garnish with fennel leaves and serve immediately.

Forgiveness is giving up hope of having had a better past.
Ann Lamot

Gelati and Pecan Praline Sauce

Serves 6.

1 qt.	vanilla ice cream, good-quality

Pecan Praline Sauce:

1 c.	heavy cream
1 c.	dark brown sugar
2 Tbs.	dark rum
1 c.	pecan halves
	Pinch of salt

1. In a heavy saucepan, combine all ingredients and cook over low heat 8 to 10 minutes, until sugar has dissolved and the texture of the sauce is silky. Do not boil.
2. Keep in refrigerator in an air-tight jar. Reheat before serving.
3. At serving time, dish out the ice cream and top with the hot praline sauce.

"I enjoy living my life fully by staying in the present time."

— Anonymous

Italian Menu #6:

An Italian Picnic

Tuscan Artichoke Spread
Red Pepper and Olive Spread
Herbed Italian Meat Loaf
Pasta Verde al Fresco
Olive Oil Mayonnaise
Mixed Greens with Gorgonzola
Stuffed Dates and Carmel Sauce

Envision sitting under a large grape arbor, overlooking vineyards as far as the eye can see. The hot Tuscan sun beats down on you, but the arbor cools you with its shade. Your party sits at a long, wood table in straight-backed, wooden chairs. A checkered tablecloth covers the table, and a large bowl of fruit sits in the center. Carafes of wine of the vineyard stand at each end of the table — both red and white, to please all palates, along with platters of these picnic dishes. Everyone lifts their glasses for a toast. Buon appetito!

Tuscan Artichoke Spread

I especially like this with sticks of fresh, raw fennel.

Serves 6 to 8.

2 jars	marinated artichoke hearts (6-oz. jars)
3	cloves garlic, crushed
1/4 to 1/3 c.	extra-virgin olive oil
1 Tbs.	fresh lemon juice
	Salt and white pepper to taste
	Fresh vegetables such as fennel, tomatoes, zucchini, mushrooms, peppers, green onions, etc.
	Crostini, crackers, or bread

1. Drain marinade off artichoke hearts and reserve for another use, such as salad dressing or on top of cooked vegetables.
2. In a food processor fitted with a metal blade, process artichoke hearts and garlic until finely chopped.
3. With motor running, dribble olive oil and lemon juice in through feed tube; continue processing until mixture is smooth and fluffy. Add salt and white pepper to taste.
4. Refrigerate till serving time. Serve the purée with vegetables, crostini, crackers, or breadsticks.

"I joyously give thanks for what I already have, what I am about to receive, and what is the greatest gift of all — the presence of God."

— Daily Word

Red Pepper and Olive Spread

Serves 6 to 8.

8 oz.	cream cheese, softened
1/3 c.	roasted red bell peppers
1 tsp.	minced garlic
Dash	freshly ground black pepper
2 cans	sliced ripe olives, well-drained (2.2-oz. cans)
2 Tbs.	chopped fresh basil

1. In food processor fitted with a metal blade, process cream cheese, roasted peppers, garlic, and black pepper till blended and smooth.
2. Remove blade from processor and stir in olives and chopped basil. Transfer to serving dish and chill until firm.
3. Serve with crackers, crostini, or thick slices of zucchini or cucumber rounds.

"One life is not worth more than another. Each life is of equal importance and value."

— D.J.

Herbed Italian Meat Loaf

This looks great when you slice it and find the surprise of the hard-cooked eggs inside. It makes a very tasty main dish for a picnic.

Serves 6 to 8.

1	small onion, chopped fine (about 1/2 c.)
3 Tbs.	extra-virgin olive oil
1 lb.	ground top sirloin (you can grind it in your food processor)
3 Tbs.	cream
	Salt and freshly ground black pepper to taste
1 Tbs.	chopped fresh tarragon, or 1 tsp. dried
1	large egg, lightly beaten
2 tsp.	tomato sauce
1/4 c.	fresh, soft bread crumbs
2	hard-cooked large eggs, shelled

1. Preheat oven to 375 degrees. Sauté chopped onion in olive oil till transparent and very lightly browned.
2. Add cooked onion to the ground beef in a bowl, together with the salt, pepper, and tarragon.
3. Add half of the beaten egg, all of the tomato sauce, the bread crumbs, and the cream, and mix well.
4. Place the hard-cooked eggs in the center of the meat mixture and mound into a loaf shape.
5. Place in shallow roasting pan and rub the top and sides with the remaining beaten egg.
6. Bake approximately 45 minutes until nicely browned. Serve hot or cold. You may garnish with Italian parsley and lots of pickled vegetables and olives, if you wish.

"Spirit, health, and giving are the most important elements of life."
— D.J.

Pasta Verde al Fresco

This is one of my very favorite pasta salads — and everyone else's too. It goes well with any variety of picnic fare or barbecued meats.

Serves 8.

1 lb.	shell or corkscrew pasta
6 to 7 qts.	water
2 Tbs.	canola or extra-virgin olive oil
2 tsp.	salt
1-1/2 c.	firmly packed, chopped fresh Italian parsley
1-1/4 c.	homemade or commercial mayonnaise
3/4 c.	plain yogurt
1 to 2	cloves garlic, minced
1 bunch	green onions, finely sliced
1/2 tsp.	celery salt
	Freshly ground black pepper to taste
1/2 tsp.	ground coriander
1/2 c.	finely chopped fresh chives, or 2 tsp. dried

1. Bring water, salt, and oil to a boil; add pasta and cook about 9 minutes or till al dente. **DO NOT OVERCOOK.**
2. Drain, place in a bowl, and cool.
3. Mince parsley in food processor. Add mayonnaise, yogurt, the minced garlic, and half of the sliced green onions.
4. Blend well till sauce is smooth and a lovely green shade.
5. Season pasta with celery salt, pepper, and coriander, and toss lightly. Add the remaining green onions and the chives.
6. Gently mix in the green sauce and taste for seasoning, adding more if necessary. Chill before serving.

My Way:

For al dente pasta take out of the simmering water one piece of pasta and taste. It should be just slightly chewy to the bite.

Olive Oil Mayonnaise

Makes about 1 cup.

1	large egg
1/2 tsp.	dry mustard
1/2 tsp.	salt
2 Tbs.	white wine vinegar
1 c.	extra-virgin olive oil, divided

1. Place the first 4 ingredients plus 1/4 c. of the olive oil in a blender, and blend at low speed to mix.
2. Uncover blender and pour in remaining 3/4 c. olive oil in a steady stream, taking no longer than 15 seconds total blending time.
3. Switch blender to high for 5 seconds and turn off.
4. Place into a container and keep in refrigerator for up to 2 weeks.

My Way:

Homemade mayonnaise is much better in flavor than commercial, so if you can make your own it's really worth it. But don't let this stop you from using ready-made. You may substitute canola oil for the olive oil if you wish.

Mixed Greens with Gorgonzola

Serves 6 to 8.

Dressing:

1	whole large egg
1	large egg yolk
3/4 tsp.	salt
	Freshly ground black pepper to taste
1/4 c.	fresh lemon juice
1 c.	canola oil
1/4 c.	extra-virgin olive oil
1	clove garlic, sliced thin
1 tsp.	dried dill weed
1 tsp.	dry mustard
1 to 2 Tbs.	creamed horseradish, or to taste
1/2 lb.	gorgonzola cheese, divided
3 Tbs.	water

Salad:

8 c.	mixed greens, washed, dried, and crisped
2	ripe Roma tomatoes, cut into wedges
1/4 c.	sliced red onion
1/2 c.	garlic croutons, homemade or packaged

Toasted pine nuts

1. In the bowl of a food processor place the whole egg and yolk, salt, pepper, and lemon juice.
2. Process, slowly pouring in the two oils until thick.
3. Add the rest of the dressing ingredients, using only half of the gorgonzola cheese. Blend well and place in a bowl. Stir in the remaining cheese and chill.
4. When ready to serve, toss dressing with greens, tomatoes, and red onion. Add croutons and toss again. Garnish with a few toasted pine nuts over the top.

"Never give up! Keep on keeping on."

— D.J.

Stuffed Dates and Caramel Sauce

This is a very simple but rich and delicious dessert, on the exotic side as desserts go. I love a little surprise like this after dinner. Ambrosia! Medjool dates are the queens of dates, and can be found in the bulk food section of specialty shops. The stuffed dates are easy to transport, however you may want to leave the sauce at home and just eat the dates with your fingers at a picnic. Serve with some Italian biscotti and hot coffee.

Serves 4; may double or triple.

1/2 c.	mascarpone cheese
1 Tbs.	grated orange zest
8 to 10	Medjool dates, pitted by slitting them down one side and easily removing the seed

Caramel Sauce:

1/4 c.	sugar
3 Tbs.	water
1/2 Tbs.	unsalted butter
1 tsp.	orange juice
1 tsp.	Grand Marnier

1. In a bowl, beat cheese until fluffy.
2. Add orange zest, and fill dates with cheese mixture.
3. Make caramel sauce: In a saucepan combine sugar with water and let stand until sugar is moistened.
4. Boil gently until mixture turns a pale golden brown. Watch carefully.
5. Remove from heat and swirl in butter, orange juice, and Grand Marnier.
6. Pour a little caramel sauce into a container or on individual plates, top with dates, and sprinkle with grated orange zest. Serve with Italian-style biscotti or amaretti cookies. Cover and chill if taking these on a picnic.

My Way:

If you don't want to make a dessert along with everything else, fresh fruit, some cheese, and/or dessert wine make a wonderful finale to this picnic. You can also add some of your own favorite confections or cookies, homemade or purchased, and still keep that Italian flavor. Enjoy!

Chapter Four

France

    In the late 1960s, French food became all the rage in the U.S. and with me as well, so I took many classes, experimented with ingredients and combinations, and prepared countless French recipes and full menus. Then I traveled to France and became a total convert to their cuisine for years to follow. I taught French cooking classes at a local kitchen shop to a steady stream of students. It is a very familiar style of cooking for me. Using the techniques and uncovering the "mysteries" of the French way with food are part of a spiritual adventure.

French Menu #1:

An Autumn Dinner, French Style

Smokes Salmon Soufflé Roll
Salade Hearts of Palm
Chicken Breasts with Red Pepper Coulis
Cumin-Scented Lentils
Pear Tart Tatin with Chantilly Cream

For some reason, this dinner tastes better to me in autumn than at any other time of the year. The soufflé as a first course works magic after being out in the cold, crisp air raking leaves or out for a walk, and then coming in, starting a fire, and preparing good things in the kitchen. The soufflé takes a little time, but the salad is easy to make with canned hearts of palm. The red pepper coulis is a fitting end-of-summer marriage with the chicken, and pears always remind me of fall. I envision this tart served by the fire with hot coffee and maybe a little snifter of brandy — a beautiful way to ground and ready the spirit for winter hibernation.

Smoked Salmon Soufflé Roll

I took of series of classes from the great cook and teacher James Beard many years ago. One of the best dishes that he taught was this first course. This recipe is also very elegant for lunch, as a main course with salad and bread.

Serves 10.

1/2 c.	toasted bread crumbs
4 Tbs.	butter
8 Tbs.	flour
2 c.	hot milk
1 tsp.	salt
1/8 tsp.	cayenne pepper
1 Tbs.	cognac
1 c. (8 oz.)	sour cream
4	large eggs, separated
1/2 lb.	smoked salmon, cut in slivers
6	green onions, chopped fine

1. Preheat oven to 325 degrees. Butter a jelly-roll pan. Line it with waxed paper, and butter the paper as well. Sprinkle with the toasted bread crumbs and set aside.
2. Melt 4 Tbs. butter in a heavy saucepan. Blend in the flour and cook until golden.
3. Take off heat, gradually add hot milk, stirring constantly.
4. Return to heat and cook, stirring, till thick. Mix in salt, pepper, cognac, and 2 Tbs. of the sour cream.
5. Remove from heat again. Lightly beat the egg yolks and mix into sauce.
6. Beat egg whites till they hold soft peaks. Fold 1/3 of the egg whites into the sauce, incorporating completely.
7. Lightly fold in remaining whites. Then spread the soufflé mixture gently into the jelly-roll pan.
8. Bake 35 to 40 minutes, or till golden and firm to the touch.
9. Remove from oven and invert the soufflé onto a clean linen tea towel. Carefully peel off the waxed paper. Trim off ends.
10. Spread roll with remaining sour cream, and sprinkle with the salmon and green onions. Roll up from long side like a jelly roll.
11. Slide onto a board or platter, using the linen towel as a sling. Cut into 1-inch slices to serve as an hors d'oeuvre or first course.

"Cooking and entertaining are expressions of something deeper."
— D.J.

Salade Hearts of Palm

Serves 6 to 8.

2	large heads butter or red lettuce
2	large tomatoes, cut into wedges
1 can	hearts of palm, drained, rinsed, and cut into 1/2-inch chunks (16-oz. can)

Dressing:

3 Tbs.	tarragon vinegar
1/2 c.	extra-virgin olive oil
3 Tbs.	minced fresh tarragon, or 1 tsp. dried
1 tsp.	salt
	White pepper to taste

1. Wash and dry the lettuce and place in a large salad bowl, tearing it into bite-size pieces.
2. Add the tomatoes and hearts of palm.
3. Mix the dressing ingredients together in a screw-top jar.
4. Pour some of the dressing over the salad, just enough to coat the greens.
5. Toss and serve.

Chicken Breasts with Red Pepper Coulis

The coulis sauce also makes a delicious spread for crostini or crackers as an appetizer.

Serves 4.

4	roasted red bell peppers, chopped very fine (for roasting tips, see "My Way" under Red Pepper Salad with Sun-Dried Tomatoes and Olives.)
3 Tbs.	extra-virgin olive oil
4	shallots, peeled and minced
1/4 c.	chopped fresh cilantro leaves
1	clove garlic, crushed
1/2 tsp.	ground cumin
1 tsp.	fresh lemon juice
	Salt and freshly ground black pepper to taste
4	large, boned and skinned chicken breast halves
2 Tbs.	butter

Sprigs of fresh mint

1. Make the coulis: Place minced roasted red peppers in a large mixing bowl. Stir, and slowly add 2 Tbs. of the olive oil, the shallots, cilantro, garlic, and cumin. Season with lemon juice; salt and pepper to taste. Mix well and set aside.
2. Prepare the chicken: Wash and dry chicken. In a large skillet over high heat, add the remaining 1 Tbs. olive oil. Add the chicken breasts and sauté 3 to 4 minutes without crowding.
3. Add butter and sauté 3 minutes more.
4. Remove pan from heat and pour off fat. Return pan to heat and turn chicken breasts.
5. Dry-sauté chicken 5 to 7 minutes, or until done. Remove chicken from pan, and season with salt and pepper to taste.
6. Divide red pepper coulis among four plates. Arrange chicken breasts on top of each pool of coulis. Garnish each plate with a sprig of fresh mint.

"There is more to life than money."
— Rosemary Woods

Cumin-Scented Lentils

Serves 4.

12 oz.	lentils
	Olive oil, for sautéing
2	cloves garlic, crushed
4	shallots, chopped fine
2 oz.	pancetta ham, or prosciutto
2	bay leaves
1 heaping Tbs.	ground cumin
	Salt to taste, about 1 tsp.

Chopped fresh cilantro

1. Wash the lentils well and set aside. Heat a small amount of olive oil in a pan and add garlic, shallots, pancetta, and bay leaves; cook over low heat until the shallots are soft and transparent.
2. Add the lentils and cumin, and stir well until they are coated with oil.
3. Add water to cover (2 to 3 c.), and salt to taste. Simmer slowly over low heat until lentils are tender, but still intact. Add more water if necessary, but not too much, since most of the liquid should be evaporated when the lentils are done.
4. To serve, drain away any excess liquid, sprinkle lentils with chopped cilantro leaves, and season to taste.

My Way:

Buy lentils in bulk in the healthy foods section of the supermarket. They are much fresher than packaged, and less expensive too.

Pear Tart Tatin with Chantilly Cream

This dessert is much easier to prepare than it looks when inverted onto a lovely silver platter. It is an impressive presentation and just as delicious. I've divided the recipe into 3 parts for easy preparation.

Serves 8.

A. Make and chill the tart pastry.

Tart pastry:

1-1/2 c.	all-purpose flour
1/4 tsp.	salt
8 Tbs.	unsalted butter, cut into bits
4 to 6 Tbs.	cold water

1. In a bowl combine flour and salt.
2. Add butter and blend with a fork until mixture resembles coarse meal.
3. Add just enough water to form the mixture into a ball.
4. Wrap in plastic wrap and chill for about 1 hour before rolling out. Makes one tart shell.

B. Make the pear filling and finish the tart.

Pear Filling:

6 Tbs.	unsalted butter
6	winter pears, peeled, cored, and halved
1 c.	sugar
2 tsp.	lemon zest
1/4 c.	water

1. Preheat oven to 400 degrees. In a large skillet over moderate heat, melt the butter.
2. Add pears, 1/2 c. of the sugar, and the lemon zest. Cook, stirring frequently, until pears start to brown and soften slightly. Transfer to a plate and let cool.
3. In a heavy saucepan over moderate heat, cook remaining 1/2 c. sugar and water, washing down the sides of the pan with a brush dipped in cold water, until the mixture is light caramel in color. Do not use a Teflon-coated pan for this procedure.
4. Immediately pour the caramel into a heavy, 9-inch metal

We do not seek love, we allow it to come to us. It is by our faith that it finds us.

Anonymous

pie pan. Tilt the pan so that the caramel coats the bottom evenly. Cool to set.

5. Arrange the pears over the caramel, cut side up, in one layer in a decorative pattern to completely cover the bottom of the pan.

6. Roll out pastry to a round that is large enough to cover pears, and place on top of fruit. Pinch edges of pastry around the rim of the pie pan.

7. Set the pan on a baking sheet, place in middle of oven, and bake 50 minutes or until pastry is golden.

8. Remove the pan from oven, and place on top of the stove over moderate heat for about 3 minutes, shaking the pan to release the pears. Loosen the edges with a spatula if necessary.

9. Invert tart onto a large enough platter to hold it with room to spare: Place the platter over the tart pan and flip over quickly, holding it over the kitchen sink to catch any drips. Serve with Chantilly Cream.

C. Whip the Chantilly Cream.

Chantilly Cream:
- 1 c. heavy cream
- 3 Tbs. powdered sugar
- 1 tsp. vanilla extract, or 1 Tbs. pear brandy

1. Beat the cream in a chilled bowl with chilled beaters until fluffy. Continue beating while adding the powdered sugar. Then add the vanilla and beat till soft peaks form. Do not overbeat.

2. Place cream in a bowl and pass separately.

"We do not belong to ourselves. We belong to the universe."
— Buckminster Fuller

French Menu #2:

A French Supper by the Fire

Melted Brie with Hazelnuts and Apples
Curry Dip and Crudités
Caesar Salad
Boeuf á la Bourguignon with Potatoes, Carrots and Mushrooms
Herbed Bentley Butter
Cherries Jubilee

Fire, one of the four elements of the universe, is especially nurturing in the wintertime when we're not able to be outside enjoying the sun and fresh air. I love to eat by firelight, which adds to the ambiance and spirit of the meal. If you don't have a fireplace, use candles; the amount of energy and light from a single candle is amazing. This menu reflects the warmth of fire, from the cozy, robust Boeuf Bourguignon with its wonderful sauce to the flaming Cherries Jubilee. These foods spell comfort to me.

Melted Brie with Hazelnuts and Apples

So easy to make, so delicious!

Serves 6 to 8.

1 wedge	Brie cheese, cut in half horizontally (8-oz.)
2 Tbs.	butter
1/4 c.	finely chopped, toasted hazelnuts
2	apples, thinly sliced (pears are equally as good)

1. Place each Brie half "skin" side down and side by side on a 10-inch, microwave-proof serving plate.
2. Place butter in a 1-cup glass measure. Microwave on high for about 20 to 30 seconds or until melted. Pour butter evenly over the Brie.
3. Sprinkle with nuts. Microwave the cheese on medium for 3 to 5 minutes. Watch carefully. The Brie should be soft enough to dip into with fruit slices.
4. Surround cheese with sliced fruit and serve.

My Way:

Toasting Hazelnuts: Place on a cookie sheet and bake in a 350-degree oven for about 15 minutes. Watch carefully so they don't burn. Turn them out onto a clean kitchen tea towel and wrap up to cool for 5 to10 minutes. Then rub the nuts together enclosed in the towel until most of the brown skin comes off. It won't all come off, but the majority will. Discard the skin and store the hazelnuts in an air-tight container in the refrigerator or freezer.

Curry Dip and Crudités

Makes about 2 cups.

2 tsp.	curry powder
1-1/2 tsp.	minced garlic
1/2 tsp.	salt
1 Tbs.	sugar
2 tsp.	prepared horseradish
1 Tbs.	finely minced shallot
2 Tbs.	cider vinegar
1 c.	sour cream
1 c.	mayonnaise

Raw vegetables cut into bite-size pieces

1. Place curry powder in a small skillet on low to moderate heat and cook 2 to 3 minutes, being careful not to burn.
2. Mix garlic, salt, sugar, horseradish, shallot, and vinegar together. Add the cooled curry powder.
3. Add sour cream and mayonnaise and mix well.
4. Cover and chill several hours or overnight.
5. Serve dip with crudités. It's also great with a seafood salad topped with toasted pine nuts.

"No one comes away from life unscathed."
— D.J.

Caesar Salad

I make fresh bread croutons a whole loaf at a time and then refrigerate the rest to have on hand when I need them. This Caesar Salad is an easier adaptation of the original.

Serves 6 to 8.

Dressing:

1/2 c.	extra-virgin olive oil
2 Tbs.	white wine vinegar
3 Tbs.	fresh lemon juice
1	large clove garlic, crushed
1 tsp.	salt
	Freshly ground black pepper to taste
1 tsp.	Dijon mustard
2 tsp.	anchovy paste
1	large egg, raw, optional
1 c.	dry bread cubes
1	large head romaine lettuce, washed, dried, and crisped
1/2 c.	Parmesan cheese

1. Preheat oven to 350 degrees. Mix all the dressing ingredients in a screw-top jar, shaking well to blend.
2. Toast bread cubes in oven for 15 to 20 minutes, spraying them with olive oil a couple of times and tossing. When they are golden brown and crisp, put them into a large bowl, toss with one or two cloves of crushed garlic and a little olive oil, and set aside to cool. Store croutons in a plastic bag in the refrigerator.
3. Tear lettuce into a salad bowl. Add the cheese.
4. Toss with as much dressing as you desire. You probably will not need it all. The salad should not be soggy. Add croutons and toss again. Serve immediately.

My Way:

Streamline Your Caesar Salad: Make the dressing in advance. It will keep for several days in the refrigerator. (I make a jar full of the dressing to have on hand for salads all week.) Put the lettuce in the salad bowl along with the grated cheese early in the day, cover with plastic wrap, and refrigerate. Toast the croutons a day or two ahead. Then all you have to do is toss and serve just before eating – much easier on your peace of mind than doing everything at once.

Boeuf a la Bourguignon with Potatoes, Carrots and Mushrooms

The best beef stew on a cold winter's night. Bacon is the secret to its great flavor. Hot bread and herbed butter served in little crocks are all you need with this hearty meal, as well as a good cabernet sauvignon wine, of course.

Serves 8.

6 slices	pepper bacon
3 lbs.	lean stew meat, or bottom chuck, cut into 2-inch pieces, any excess fat trimmed away
	Salt and freshly ground black pepper to taste
	Flour, for dredging meat
	Reserved bacon fat plus canola oil as needed, for sautéing
2	carrots, sliced
2	large onions, coarsely chopped
2	cloves garlic, minced
2 to 3	Tbs. flour
2 to 3 c.	beef stock
2 c.	Burgundy wine (good but not expensive)
2 Tbs.	tomato paste
3/4 tsp.	thyme
1	bay leaf

Accompaniments:

24	small onions, parboiled (canned ones are O.K.)
1 lb.	carrots, cooked al dente
1 lb.	fresh button mushrooms, sautéed in butter
18 to 20	small, whole red potatoes, cooked until just tender (leave skins on)

Chopped fresh Italian parsley

1. Preheat oven to 325 degrees. Sauté the bacon till crisp in a large Dutch oven pot. Remove and reserve the bacon; pour the fat into a small bowl and reserve separately.

2. Pat meat pieces dry with a paper towel. Sprinkle them with salt and pepper, and toss with enough flour to lightly coat. Add a Tbs. or two of the bacon fat to the same pot, and sauté a few pieces of beef at a time till

My Way:

Meat will not brown well if it is too moist or if you crowd the pan with too much at once. The moisture ends up steaming the meat. Pat meat dry with a paper towel before sautéing. The resulting brown bits from the sauté pan intensify the flavor of the sauce.

brown on all sides. Don't crowd the pan (see "My Way," below), and be careful not to burn the beef. Remove to a plate and continue to brown the rest of the meat pieces, adding more bacon fat, or canola oil if you run out of fat, as needed.

3. After all the meat is browned and removed from the pan, sauté the sliced carrots and chopped onions along with the minced garlic. Brown lightly for 5 minutes, then return to the pot with the vegetables and stir to blend.

4. Add all of the beef stock and wine to the meat mixture. The liquid should just barely cover the meat and vegetables. Stir in tomato paste and herbs. Bring to a simmer on top of the stove, then cover and bake in preheated oven for 2 to 3 hours. Check after 2 hours or so. When the meat is tender, the stew is done. Meat should not be falling apart but must be very tender.

5. Meanwhile, prepare the accompaniments: Sauté the whole onions in butter to brown lightly. Sauté the mushrooms separately on high in a little oil or butter till golden brown but still firm. Cook the carrots and the potatoes separately in about 2 inches of water, simmering gently. Chop the bacon.

6. When meat is tender, place a large strainer over a saucepan and strain the meat sauce into it.

7. Wash casserole out and return just the meat to it, discarding the cooked-out vegetables. Skim fat from the sauce and simmer 5 minutes to enhance flavor. The sauce should lightly coat a spoon. If too thick, add more stock or red wine. If too thin, boil down rapidly before you add the meat. You may also add 1 Tbs. cornstarch mixed with a little water to thicken the sauce slightly.

8. Add the bacon and the accompanying cooked vegetables to the hot stew, stirring gently with a rubber spatula so as to not break up the vegetables. Correct seasoning. Thoroughly heat through, but do not boil. Serve in large, shallow, soup-type bowls, garnished with chopped fresh parsley, with plenty of hot bread and butter.

Herbed Bentley Butter

Makes about 1 cup. Freezes well.

1 c.	butter, softened
2 Tbs.	finely chopped pimiento or roasted red peppers
1 Tbs.	chopped chives or green onion tops
1 tsp.	Worcestershire sauce
1 tsp.	minced garlic
1/2 tsp.	salt

1. Beat butter in medium-sized bowl till creamy. Gently and gradually stir in remaining ingredients, beating continually to incorporate.
2. Transfer into a crock or individual crocks and chill well. Keeps in refrigerator for 5 days. Serve with hot French bread.

"It seems sometimes that changing ourselves is even more difficult than changing the world."

— Anonymous

Cherries Jubilee

A very special but simple-to-make dessert that stands up to this hearty menu. After all the time you've spent making the bourguignon, you deserve an effortless but elegant dessert.

Serves 8.

1 can	pitted black cherries (2-1/2 lbs.)
2 Tbs.	sugar
1/3 c.	brandy, heated
1/3 c.	Kirsch liqueur, heated
1 qt.	good-quality vanilla ice cream

1. Pour 3/4 of the liquid from the cherries into a skillet.
2. Add the sugar, stir, and place over moderate heat.
3. Heat the two liquors together in the microwave to hot, not boiling.
4. Add cherries to the skillet and heat through.
5. Add the heated liquors to the pan and flame them (carefully), shaking the pan gently to move the alcohol around and burn it off. After the flames subside, the sauce is done.
6. Scoop ice cream into bowls and spoon some of the Cherries Jubilee over the top.

"I accept and love myself totally, even with all the mistakes I have made in life."

— D.J.

French Menu #3:

Springtime in Paris

Miniature Quiches with Smoked Salmon and Dill
Asparagus Soup
Sautéed Chicken Breasts and Artichoke-Chive Sauce
Rice and Pepper Pilaf
Lemon Blossom Tart

Here's a lovely little French dinner that is relatively easy on the cook. Again, a lot can be made ahead and frozen or refrigerated. The lemon tart is especially popular. A nice, chilled, medium-dry white wine complements this menu from appetizer to dessert. Celebrate spring, and all of the promise of abundance from Mother Earth that it brings, with this dinner. As you sit around the table with family or friends, take the time to plan how to nurture the spirit for the coming of spring and summer.

Miniature Quiches with Smoked Salmon and Dill

Three easy steps to an impressive appetizer.

Serves 8.

A. Prepare the quiche shells.

Pastry:

3 oz.	cream cheese, at room temperature
1/2 c.	unsalted butter
1 c.	flour

1. Preheat oven to 375 degrees. Cream the cheese and butter together; add flour and mix well. Divide into twelve 1-inch balls.
2. Place and shape into sides and bottom of miniature muffin tins. Cover and chill while you make the filling.
3. Prebake the empty shells for 10 minutes. Cool slightly.

B. Make the salmon filling.

Filling:

1/2 lb.	smoked salmon, flaked
1 Tbs.	fresh dill, finely chopped

1. In a small bowl, mix together the flaked salmon and the chopped dill and set aside.

C. Make the custard and complete the quiche.

Custard:

3/4 c.	light cream
3/4 c.	heavy cream
4	large eggs
	Salt and freshly ground black pepper to taste
1/4 tsp.	fresh grated nutmeg, or to taste

1. Preheat oven to 375 degrees. Whisk cream and eggs together thoroughly. Add the seasoning to taste. This makes enough custard to fill one 10-inch quiche or sixteen 2-inch tarts.

"You are a child of the universe no less than the trees and the stars;

You have a right to be here.

And whether or not it is clear to you,

No doubt the universe is unfolding as it should."

— Anonymous

2. Place 2 tsp. of salmon-dill mixture in each tart and pour enough custard into each shell to reach just below edge of pastry.

3. Bake miniature quiches for 10 to 15 minutes or until filling is puffed and lightly golden brown; bake longer for one large tart. Serve immediately, or you may bake and freeze, and then rebake them frozen at 350 degrees for about 15 to 20 minutes.

Asparagus Soup

This is a classic soup for springtime when asparagus is in abundance. It freezes well.

Serves 8.

2-1/2 lbs.	asparagus
2 Tbs.	butter
1/2 c.	minced yellow onion
1/4 c.	minced fresh Italian parsley
1-1/2 tsp.	ground coriander
3 Tbs.	flour
6 c.	chicken stock, heated
2 Tbs.	fresh lemon juice
	Salt and white pepper to taste

Lemon slices, for garnish
Minced fresh Italian parsley, for garnish

1. Snap off the tough, bottom parts of asparagus and discard. Steam the spears till al dente; they should still be bright green, but the point of a knife should go into a spear easily.
2. Cut tips of spears off and reserve. Cut the rest of the asparagus into large chunks.
3. In a large saucepan sauté the onion, parsley, and coriander in the butter until vegetables are soft but not brown.
4. Add the flour and cook mixture, stirring for 3 minutes. Do not let the mixture get brown. You only want to cook the flour so that the soup will not have a starchy taste.
5. Remove from heat and add the chicken stock, stirring to blend with a wire whisk. Heat and simmer 5 minutes.
6. Remove pan from heat and add asparagus stalk pieces. Purée the mixture in blender until smooth.
7. Rinse out the saucepan and pour the purée back into it. Then add the cream and reserved asparagus tips. Heat through to hot, but do not boil.
8. Stir in lemon juice, salt, and pepper. Serve soup garnished with a floating lemon slice and sprinkled with minced parsley.

Darkness has no power on existence in the light.
Anonymous

Sautéed Chicken Breasts and Artichoke-Chive Sauce

Serves 6.

1 bunch	green onions, cleaned, trimmed, and cut into slivers
1 can	artichoke hearts, in water, hearts drained and cut in half
1 Tbs.	fresh lemon juice
1 tsp.	grated lemon zest
2 Tbs.	butter
1/4 c.	flour
1 tsp.	salt
	Freshly ground black pepper
3	whole chicken breasts, skinned, boned, flattened slightly, and then halved
3 Tbs.	butter
3/4 c.	chicken stock

Sauce:

1/2 c.	chopped celery
1	medium onion, finely chopped
2 c.	chicken stock
3 Tbs.	flour
	Salt and freshly ground black pepper to taste

Minced green onion tops, for garnish

1. Sauté onions in 2 Tbs. butter for 2 or 3 minutes. Add artichoke hearts, lemon juice, and grated zest, and heat through. Set aside.
2. Mix 1/4 c. flour, salt, and pepper; coat the chicken breasts with this mixture.
3. Sauté chicken in 3 Tbs. butter over medium-high heat, turning when light golden on each side.
4. Add chicken stock, heat to boiling, then reduce heat to simmer lightly for 5 to 10 minutes. Remove chicken and keep warm.
5. Make the sauce: In the same pan sauté the celery and the chopped onion in 2 Tbs. canola oil for about 5 minutes. Add the flour and cook 2 to 3 minutes longer.
6. Heated chicken stock in the microwave. Stir it into the sauce with a whisk to prevent lumping.

"We need a lift from daily life. One way to do this is by giving and sharing ourselves, our talents, our homes."

— D.J.

7. Place all in the food processor and process to a smooth sauce.

8. Place the sauce back in the pan and keep warm until ready to serve. Just before serving add the artichoke hearts and heat through. Correct seasoning. Place a chicken breast on a plate and nap some of the sauce over it. Garnish with the minced green onion tops.

Rice and Pepper Pilaf

Combining sautéed vegetables with rice adds both color and nourishment, as well as unusual appeal. It makes life easy on the cook, since you won't need to fool with an extra vegetable dish.

Serves 6.

1/4 c.	canola oil
1	medium onion, chopped
1	medium green bell pepper, cut into slivers
1	medium red bell pepper, cut into slivers
1	clove garlic, minced
1 tsp.	salt
5 c.	chicken stock
1-1/4 c.	long-grain white rice
1-1/4 c.	wild rice
1/2 tsp.	thyme
1 tsp.	marjoram
1/2 tsp.	beau monde seasoning
2 Tbs.	butter

1. Sauté the onion and the garlic in half the oil. In another skillet sauté the peppers for 3 to 4 minutes and set them aside.
2. To the onion and garlic add the salt, chicken stock, rice, and the herbs.
3. Bring to a boil and stir once. Cover and simmer 25 to 35 minutes or till rice is done and all liquid is absorbed. Add 2 Tbs. butter and stir gently. Add half the peppers to the cooked rice and stir again.
4. Garnish with the remaining peppers on top of the rice and serve immediately.

Lemon Blossom Tart

Easy and delicious! Great to take on a picnic or a potluck, too.

Serves 8.

4	large eggs, unbeaten
6 Tbs.	butter, melted
1/4 c.	milk
	Zest of 2 lemons, grated (yellow part only — the white part is too bitter to use)
1-3/4 c.	sugar
1 Tbs.	flour
2 Tbs.	fine yellow cornmeal
1/4 tsp.	salt
1/4 c.	fresh lemon juice
	Powdered sugar
1	partially baked pie shell
1	large egg white, lightly beaten

1. Preheat oven to 375 degrees. Place all ingredients in a bowl except for the pie crust and the powdered sugar.
2. Paint the partially baked pie shell with the lightly beaten egg white. This prevents the liquid from soaking through the crust. Prebake crust for 10 minutes.
3. Pour the lemon filling into the prebaked crust and slide it back into the oven. Bake for 30 to 35 minutes more, then test with a knife blade. If it comes out clean, the custard is done.
4. Cool. Sprinkle with sifted powdered sugar and serve.

*

"There is great joy in living by giving."

— D.J.

French Menu #4:

Dinner Napoleon

Walnut Mushroom Pâté
Tossed Greens in Classic French Vinaigrette
Chicken and Shrimp Morengo
Parslied Red Potatoes
Chocolate Mousse á L'Orange

I became intrigued with Napoleon when I visited his tomb in Paris. He was an interesting historical character, to say the least. He was small in stature, but I'm sure he had a big spirit (and ego too!). It helps me to remember that spirit holds much more than what our physical appearance shows, and reminds me to look inward to discover the treasures that are there. The treasures in this menu, filled with deceptively simple ingredients, are in the flavor combinations.

Walnut Mushroom Pâté

A beautiful student gave me this recipe many years ago. I make it often, especially around the holidays. This recipe makes a large portion but freezes well. Keep some in the fridge for up to a week and freeze the rest for entertaining or a spur-of-the-moment picnic — to give you peace of mind and keep your spirit intact!

Serves 12 or more.

4 Tbs.	butter
4 c.	chopped fresh white mushrooms
1/2 c.	chopped green onions (white part only)
1/2 tsp.	thyme
1 tsp.	salt
1/3 c.	sherry
8 oz.	cream cheese, softened (you may use low-fat, but it won't set up as well)
1 c.	finely chopped walnuts, toasted (see "My Way," below)
1/4 c.	chopped fresh Italian parsley
	Dash Tabasco sauce
1/4 c.	minced green onion tops, for garnish

1. In a heavy skillet melt butter over moderate heat. Add the mushrooms, white part of green onions, and thyme.
2. Cook, stirring until green onions are transparent and all of the liquid from the mushrooms has evaporated, about 5 to 8 minutes.
3. Add salt and sherry and cook till liquid is almost evaporated. Remove from heat, and cool.
4. Mix softened cream cheese and mushroom mixture in a large bowl. Stir and blend thoroughly.
5. Stir in walnuts, parsley, and Tabasco. Place into a serving dish or small crocks. Chill, covered, at least 2 hours. Sprinkle top with green onion tops or parsley. Serve with crackers or crostini.

My Way:

Toasting Walnuts: Simmering walnuts in water removes any characteristic bitterness and brings out the nutty flavor of the walnuts, especially once they are toasted. Keep all nuts in the freezer so they'll stay fresh.

1. Preheat oven to 350 degrees. Place walnuts in a pot of water to cover.
2. Bring to a boil on stove, reduce heat, and simmer 5 minutes.
3. Strain in sieve and rinse away all the scum that forms.
4. Pour nuts onto an ungreased cookie sheet with sides on it.
5. Toast in oven for 10 to 15 minutes or until golden. Be careful not to get them too brown.
6. Store in the refrigerator or freezer for garnish, salads, or dessert topping.

Tossed Greens in Classic French Vinaigrette

This vinaigrette recipe can be doubled, tripled, or made in larger batches. All you have to do is the math! I make a large container full and keep it in the refrigerator for a week or two at a time. Pour a little of this dressing plus some herbs and chopped nuts or cheese over a chicken breast and bake for a quick, simple dinner.

Serves 2 to 4.

Basic Vinaigrette:

3 Tbs.	extra-virgin olive oil or canola oil, or a combination of the two
1 Tbs.	white vinegar, or fresh lemon juice
1/2 tsp.	Dijon mustard
1/4 tsp.	salt
	Freshly ground black pepper to taste
1/2	head lettuce or a mixture of greens, washed, dried, and crisped
	Salad vegetables of your choice

1. Make the dressing: The old-fashioned way is to place all ingredients except the oil in a bowl, then slowly whisk in the oil. Instead, I place all of the ingredients in a screw-top jar and shake well. To this basic recipe you may add garlic and/or any herb that you wish. Try using lemon or lime juice or zest, balsamic vinegar, or any type of seasoned vinegar in place of the white wine vinegar for variety. Add a dash of sugar, or a Tbs. or two of crème fraiche or sour cream, or perhaps bits of fine diced peppers, green onions or chives, salsa, capers, etc. Experiment!

2. Prepare the lettuce and any type of vegetables that can be eaten raw or par-cooked. Place all in a bowl and chill till just before serving.

3. Toss salad with the dressing until just coated, not soggy. Serve immediately. You may also add croutons or toasted nuts of any kind. Toss these in just at the end or use as garnish over the top.

Chicken and Shrimp Morengo

This dish is said to have been Napoleon's favorite. I serve it with small red potatoes, but it is also good with steamed rice.

Serves 6 to 8.

1/4 c.	extra-virgin olive oil
1	fryer (3-1/2 lbs.), cut into parts, washed, and dried
	Salt and freshly ground black pepper to taste
3	cloves garlic, crushed
5	large, ripe tomatoes
1 c.	dry white wine
8	large, cooked shrimp
8	whole mushrooms
	Butter for sautéing
1/4 c.	minced fresh Italian parsley
	Juice of one lemon
2 tsp.	lemon zest
	Slices of lemon

1. Heat oil in a skillet and sauté chicken pieces till golden brown on all sides, sprinkling them with salt and pepper as you go. Do not crowd the pan.
2. Pour off all but 2 Tbs. of the oil and add the garlic, tomatoes, and wine.
3. Continue simmering till chicken pieces are tender, about 20 to 30 minutes.
4. Shell and devein the shrimp. Sauté in a small amount of olive oil till pink and just cooked through.
5. Sauté the mushrooms in a little butter till golden brown.
6. When chicken is cooked, add the shrimp and mushrooms to it and stir to completely heat through.
7. Place on a platter and garnish with parsley and lemon juice, lemon zest, and slices of lemon. Serve immediately with cooked red potatoes and fried bread.

Build a Better World

"'Build a better world,' God said. And I answered, 'How? The world is such a vast place, and so complicated now, and I'm small and useless. There's nothing I can do.'

But God, in all his wisdom said, 'Just build a better you.'"

— Anonymous

Parslied Red Potatoes

Serves 6 to 8.

16	small red potatoes, scrubbed and left whole
1 tsp.	salt
1 Tbs.	butter
3 Tbs.	minced fresh Italian parsley

1. Cook the potatoes in a small amount of water with the salt until just cooked through but not mushy. Test with the point of a sharp knife.
2. Drain the potatoes. Melt the butter in a sauté pan and brown the potatoes, adding more salt if needed.
3. Garnish with the parsley and serve at once with the Chicken and Shrimp Morengo.

Chocolate Mousse á L'Orange

This is the easiest mousse recipe I have ever come across, and it's delicious. I've adapted it from my friend Virginia Plainfield's recipe.

Serves 8.

3/4 c.	low-fat (2%) milk
1 c.	semisweet chocolate chips, such as Nestle brand
2 Tbs.	sugar
1 Tbs.	orange liqueur
1 tsp.	grated orange zest
	Dash salt
1	large egg

1. Scald the milk and set aside.
2. Put chocolate chips, sugar, liqueur, orange zest, salt, and milk into a blender. Blend at low speed until the chocolate chips are all melted by the hot milk.
3. Add the egg and continue to blend for 1 minute or until smooth.
4. Pour into small serving cups and chill. You may top with a dollop of whipped cream and a candied violet or some orange zest.

"When I am aware of my Spirit, I am at peace knowing to watch, and listen for guidance from my higher power."

— Anonymous

French Menu #5:

An Elegant Seafood Dinner, French Style

Roquefort Grapes
Rumaki
Tossed Greens and Hazelnuts with Cognac Dressing
Coquilles Saint Jacques
Duchesse Potatoes
Chocolate Ganache-Stuffed Crêpes

Scallops are the stars in this menu. The fruits de mer are prepared in France with large sea scallops that are sweet and succulent. I like to serve this classic French dish in real scallop shells because they remind me of the sea from which they have come, helping me to connect with nature and the mysteries of the deep.

Roquefort Grapes

From Marlene Zworowsky's cooking class.

Serves 12 or more as an hors d'oeuvre.

10 oz.	pecans
8 oz.	cream cheese (regular, not low-fat)
2 oz.	Roquefort or gorgonzola cheese
2 Tbs.	heavy cream
1 lb.	seedless green or red grapes, washed and drained

1. Preheat oven to 350 degrees. Toast the nuts in oven for about 5 minutes. Be careful not to burn.
2. Chop toasted nuts rather coarsely. Spread on a platter.
3. In bowl of food processor combine cheeses and cream; process until smooth.
4. Drop clean, dry grapes into cheese mixture and gently stir by hand to coat them. Any leftover cheese mixture can be frozen and reused.
5. Roll coated grapes in the chopped nuts and place on a tray lined with waxed paper. Chill until ready to serve.

Rumaki

You may substitute shrimp for the chicken livers, or scallops when you're not serving a scallop main course.

Serves 8.

3/4 lb.	chicken livers
	Juice of 1 lime
1 lb.	bacon, sliced and sautéed for 3 to 4 minutes to remove some of the fat (but it should still be limp), drained well
1 can	whole water chestnuts
	Salt and freshly ground black pepper

1. Preheat oven to 350 degrees. Rinse chicken livers, cut them in half, and drain on a paper towel. Sprinkle lightly with some fresh lime juice.
2. Cut bacon into half-slices. Cut water chestnuts in half.
3. Salt and pepper the chicken liver halves. Wrap bacon around a liver with a halved water chestnut piece in the center. Secure with a toothpick.
4. Bake on a rack in baking pan, about 25 to 30 minutes or until bacon is very crisp.
5. Drain and serve while hot.

"Life is more than food, and the body is more than clothing."

— D.J.

Tossed Greens and Hazelnuts with Cognac Dressing

French croissants and herbed butter go well on the side with this salad.

Serves 6.

Dressing:

1/2 c.	canola oil
1/4 c.	low-fat yogurt
1/4 c.	low-fat mayonnaise
1 Tbs.	minced green onions
1/2 tsp.	freshly ground black pepper
1/2 tsp.	salt
1	small clove garlic, crushed
Dash	Worcestershire sauce
Dash	Tabasco sauce
1 Tbs.	cognac, or other good-quality brandy
1 Tbs.	fresh lemon juice
	Mixed salad greens, about 6 c., packaged or fresh
1/3 c.	chopped toasted hazelnuts

1. In a screw-top jar combine all of the dressing ingredients except cognac and lemon juice. Blend well.
2. Mix in the cognac and lemon juice.
3. Cover and refrigerate till serving time.
4. Rinse the mixed greens. Dry well and place in a salad bowl.
5. Toss gently with enough dressing to coat the greens. Top with the chopped hazelnuts and serve immediately.

To the best of one's ability is good enough.

D.J.

Coquilles Saint Jacques

This classic French dish can be served as a first course or a main entrée. I like to prepare it in natural scallop shells. If you can't find any shells, individual, oven-proof ramekins will do. When serving Coquilles St. Jacques as a first course, skip the topping of Duchesse Potatoes.

Serves 6.

Court Bouillon: (fish stock)

1/2 c.	water
1/2 c.	dry white wine
2 sprigs	Italian parsley
1	small onion, studded with 4 whole cloves
1/4 tsp.	thyme
1/2 tsp.	salt
	Dash white pepper

Scallops and Sauce:

2 lbs.	large, fresh sea scallops, rinsed well
5 Tbs.	butter, divided
3 Tbs.	flour
3/4 c.	light cream
2	large egg yolks
	Salt and freshly ground black pepper
1/2 lb.	fresh mushrooms
2 Tbs.	fresh lemon juice
6 Tbs.	grated Parmesan cheese
	Buttered, toasted bread crumbs

1. Preheat oven to 350 degrees. For court bouillon: Place water, wine, parsley, onion, thyme, salt, and pepper in a saucepan. Bring to a simmer and cook for 5 minutes.
2. Add rinsed scallops and let sit in lightly simmering court bouillon for 5 minutes, but do not boil.
3. Strain bouillon, reserving 1 c., and place scallops in buttered ramekins or scallop shells.
4. Melt 3 Tbs. of the butter and add the flour. Cook 1 minute, then slowly add the reserved 1 c. of court bouillon. Add the cream and cook, stirring, till smooth and thick.
5. Beat egg yolks and add a little sauce to them, then add egg mixture to sauce and cook lightly for 1 minute but do not bring to a boil.

"Try to be as free as you can."

— D.J.

6. Taste and add salt and pepper if necessary; then pour some of the sauce over the scallops in their individual dishes.

7. Sauté the sliced mushrooms in 2 Tbs. butter. When golden brown, add 2 Tbs. lemon juice and blend into mushrooms. Add some of the mixture to each scallop dish.

8. Pipe around the edges with Duchesse Potatoes if desired.

9. Top with the cheese and bread crumbs and bake 10 minutes. Serve at once.

Duchesse Potatoes

Serves 6.

3	large Idaho potatoes (about 1-1/2 lbs. total), peeled
3 Tbs.	butter
1	whole large egg
2	large egg yolks
1/4 tsp.	freshly grated nutmeg
1 tsp.	salt
1/4 tsp.	white pepper
2 Tbs.	melted butter, for topping

1. Preheat oven to 400 degrees. Boil potatoes in salted water on stovetop about 20 minutes or until tender. Drain well.
2. Shake the pan over heat to remove excess water and dry the potatoes out.
3. Add 2 Tbs. butter and mash well with a potato masher.
4. Beat egg and yolks together and mix in with masher. Season and mix with wooden spoon until fluffy.
5. Put in a pastry bag fitted with a large tube (5A).
6. Pipe either in a border around platter or around ramekins, or into 2-inch puffs on a cookie sheet. Sprinkle with the melted butter.
7. Bake 20 minutes. Tops should be golden brown. If they are not, place under broiler for a very brief time.

"My life is transformed through freedom of Spirit."
— *The Daily Word*

Chocolate Ganache-Stuffed Crêpes

I know you've always wanted to make ganache, so here it is. Another great three-part dessert that's worth the effort. The unfilled crêpes can be frozen, though they are best fresh. No one but you will probably know the difference!

For more crêpe tips, see "My Way."

Makes about 2 dozen dessert crêpes. Serves 6.

A. Make the crêpes.

Crêpe Batter:

1/4 c.	butter, melted
1-1/2 c.	milk
4	large eggs
1 c.	sifted all-purpose flour
2 Tbs.	brandy
1 Tbs.	sugar

1. Melt butter and set aside to cool.
2. Beat together eggs and milk.
3. Add flour, brandy, and sugar; then add the cooled butter. Let batter stand at room temperature 30 minutes or longer.
4. Place crêpe pan over medium-high heat.
5. Add just enough batter to the pan to coat it thinly on the bottom. Use 1/4-cup measure filled half full to pour it into the pan (but you may not need it all.) Cook on first side till golden brown and edges start to curl.
6. Flip over and cook 30 seconds on second side. Remove to a plate and continue cooking the rest of the crêpes.

B. Make the ganache filling.

Chocolate Ganache:

1 1b.	semisweet chocolate chips, Nestle or Girardelli
2 c.	heavy cream

1. In a heavy saucepan, melt the chocolate chips with the cream and cook over very low heat until mixture is smooth and glossy.

My Way:

Making crêpes is truly an exercise in letting go. I always end up throwing out the first few, but then I get the gist of it and all goes well. If you or I were to make them every day by the dozens, they'd be perfect, but remember we're not into perfection, only excellence. So let go and enjoy the process.

You'll feel like you've really accomplished a work of art when you see those crêpes all stacked up on a plate in front of you – instant gratification! You don't need to worry about them sticking together since they will come apart one by one, just as they're supposed to.

2. Remove mixture to a bowl and beat (with an electric beater), until it becomes thick and of a spreading consistency, 10 minutes or longer. To thicken faster, place bowl in larger bowl of ice water and beat with a hand mixer. Makes approximately 4 cups.

C. Prepare the berry sauce and finish the dessert.

Berry Sauce:
1 pint	raspberries, fresh or frozen
1/4 c.	sherry
3/4 c.	red currant jelly

1. Blend the wine and jelly together.
2. Cook over low heat, stirring until smooth.
3. Combine with the berries and chill. You may strain the sauce if you wish but it's not imperative. May substitute strawberries for the raspberries.
4. Spoon 1 to 2 Tbs. of the ganache onto the center of a crêpe and roll it up. Place seam side down on individual dessert plates, two per person. Top with berry sauce and garnished with a sprinkling of toasted, slivered almonds if you wish. Serve immediately.

French Menu #6:

A Summer Dinner in the French Countryside

Smoked Salmon Pâté
Cognac Mushroom Soup
Barbecued Butterfly Leg of Lamb
Potatoes Anna
Marinated Vegetable Batons
Mixed Berry Charlotte

A French summer dinner, served outdoors with the moonlight and stars shining down on you and your guests, is a perfect way to welcome the summer season. Let everyone choose a favorite song, and have a sing-along afterwards. Singing together is a wonderful way to share spirit.

If you want to make this menu really easy, forget the potatoes and vegetable batons. Just make Oven-Roasted Vegetables, which you'll find in the Pacific Northwest section of this book, and serve a tossed salad instead.

Smoked Salmon Pâté

This pâté is nice because you can use canned salmon from your pantry and fix it in a flash. You don't need to use smoked salmon, thanks to the liquid smoke. If you do want to use smoked salmon instead, omit the liquid smoke. This pâté freezes well.

Serves 6 to 8.

8 oz.	cream cheese, at room temperature
3/4 tsp.	dried dill weed
1 can	red salmon (7-3/4 oz. can)
1 tsp.	liquid smoke
2 tsp.	fresh lemon juice
1/4 tsp.	Tabasco sauce

Minced fresh Italian parsley

1. Place cream cheese and dried dill in food processor and process till smooth.
2. Add remaining ingredients and process till smooth.
3. Garnish the pâté with minced parsley and serve with water biscuits or other mild crackers, crostini, or French baguette.

Give until it hurts.
Mother Theresa

Cognac Mushroom Soup

This soup freezes well, or you may refrigerate it for up to 3 days. However, add the cognac only just before serving. If you don't have good French cognac on hand, buy a small 2-oz. bottle at the liquor store, and then you won't break the bank.

Serves 8 as a first course.

3/4 lb.	whole mushrooms
1	medium onion
1	stalk celery
4 Tbs.	butter
1/4 c.	flour
5 to 6 c.	chicken stock
1-1/2 c.	light cream
	Salt and freshly ground black pepper to taste
	Cayenne pepper to taste
4 Tbs.	cognac
24	thin slices raw mushrooms, for garnish
	Paprika
2 Tbs.	minced green onion tops

1. Clean and chop the mushrooms, onions, and celery together very fine in food processor.
2. Melt butter in large, heavy pot. Stir in chopped mushrooms, onion, and celery; cook 10 minutes over medium heat, stirring occasionally.
3. Stir in flour and cook 2 minutes longer.
4. Remove pan from heat and whisk in the chicken stock and cream, smoothing out any lumps from the thickening process.
5. Return pan to heat and bring mixture to a simmer, then simmer gently 30 minutes.
6. Season soup to taste with salt, pepper, and cayenne. Remove pan from heat and add cognac to taste.
7. Garnish each serving with a few slices of raw mushrooms. Sprinkle with paprika and green onion tops, and serve immediately.

"Love people not things."
— Anonymous

Barbecued Butterfly Leg of Lamb

This recipe was given to me by my dear friend and mentor, Virginia Plainfield. If you love lamb as I do you won't find a better way to prepare it. Even those who are a little unsure about lamb really enjoy it prepared this way. Have your butcher bone and butterfly the leg of lamb.

Serves 8 to 10.

Marinade:

1/2 c.	soy sauce
1/3 c.	brown sugar
3 Tbs.	canola oil
	Juice of 1 lemon
3 Tbs.	dry red wine
1	large clove garlic, minced
1 Tbs.	minced fresh rosemary, or 1 tsp. dried

1 (6-lb.)	leg of lamb, butterflied (about 4-1/2 lbs., boned) and trimmed of the tough part on the outside, called the fell

Admit. Accept. Adapt. Advocate. Achieve.

1. Combine marinade ingredients in a saucepan. Heat through, then set aside to cool.
2. Place the butterflied leg of lamb flat in a stainless steel or glass pan with the marinade. Cover and refrigerate at least 4 hours.
3. Start a charcoal fire. Drain the lamb and reserve the marinade. When coals are hot, barbecue lamb for approximately 20 to 30 minutes per side, basting often with the reserved marinade. Check for doneness.
4. Slice on the diagonal and serve immediately with a good quality mint jelly, or make an extra batch of the marinade and, after it's boiled, put it aside to use as a sauce with the lamb. Do not use the marinade that came in contact with the raw lamb as a sauce.

Potatoes Anna

There is never any of this dish left over!

Serves 6 to 8.

3/4 c.	butter (1-1/2 cubes)
3 to 4	large baking potatoes
	Salt and freshly ground black pepper
1 Tbs.	minced chives

Chopped fresh Italian parsley

1. Preheat oven to 450 degrees. Melt 2 Tbs. butter in an oven-proof skillet. Swirl to coat sides. Keep the rest of the butter chilled and at hand.
2. Peel and slice potatoes thin and dry them well.
3. Make a single layer of potatoes, creating an overlapping spiral, starting from the center and working outward, all up the sides of the pan.
4. Sprinkle layer generously with salt and freshly ground black pepper and chives.
5. Cut butter into small bits and scatter some of it on this layer.
6. Continue this process of layering till pan is full. Cover pan tightly, first with aluminum foil, then press down and cover with a heavy pan lid.
7. Heat pan on high on top of stove till sizzling, about five minutes or so. You want the bottom layer of potatoes to be nicely dark browned but not burnt. (This is the only tricky part, you'll have to trust your instincts. It's all part of the drama.)
8. Place in lower part of oven and bake for 30 minutes or till the potatoes are tender.
9. Let cool 1 minute. Work a rubber spatula around edge and onto the bottom to loosen potatoes as much as possible. Place a round serving platter over the pan and invert the Potatoes Anna onto the platter. Sprinkle with parsley and serve immediately.

"Believe in yourself, you're worth it!"

— D.J.

Marinated Vegetables Batons

A different way to present a vegetable course.

Serves 6 to 8.

Dressing:

3 Tbs.	extra-virgin olive oil
3 Tbs.	canola oil
2 Tbs.	fresh lemon juice
1 tsp.	grated lemon zest (yellow part only)
2 Tbs.	minced green onion
1 tsp.	minced capers
1/2 tsp.	salt
1/4 tsp.	white pepper
2	beets
1/4 lb.	green beans
2	small zucchini
2	carrots
2	turnips

1. Place all the dressing ingredients in a screw-top jar and shake well. Chill until serving time.
2. Peel and prepare all the vegetables and cut into 2-inch long "sticks" that are 1/2 inch wide.
3. Bring 3 c. water to a boil. Place vegetable steamer over water.
4. Steam all the vegetables individually for 3 minutes or till tender.
5. Drain and rinse quickly with cold water. Drain thoroughly and reserve.
6. Arrange on a rectangular serving platter and drizzle the dressing over all. Serve immediately.

Mixed Berry Charlotte

The best time to prepare this recipe is in the summer, with the abundance of fresh berries; however, served at Christmas time using frozen berries, it is a stunning display with its bright, ruby red color. The flavorful berries are a perfect ending to this meal.

Serves 10.

8 to 10	thin slices good-quality, day-old white bread, crusts trimmed
3/4 c.	sugar
2 lbs.	mixed fresh blueberries, raspberries, and blackberries, or about 5 c. of frozen, some juice removed

Whipped cream

1. Cut a circle of bread to fit the bottom of a 3-cup charlotte mold or a bowl with a round bottom.
2. Butter the bottom of the mold. Line remainder of mold with wedge-shaped pieces of bread, pressing firmly and leaving no gaps. Reserve several pieces to cover the top.
3. In a medium saucepan over low heat, dissolve sugar in 3 Tbs. of water.
4. Add berries and cook 3 to 5 minutes. Remove from heat and strain off 1 c. of the juice and set aside.
5. Turn fruit mixture into prepared mold. There should be plenty of liquid but not so it's runny. Cover with the remaining bread.
6. Place a saucer on top of pudding and press down on it with a weight. Chill overnight.
7. In a small saucepan over medium heat, boil reserved juice till it reduces and becomes syrupy. Cool.
8. To serve, remove weight and saucer from the charlotte. Place serving plate over it and invert pudding onto a pretty serving plate, preferably with 1-inch sides.
9. Pour the syrup over the top, letting it drip down the sides. If there is any syrup left, serve it on the side, along with the whipped cream.

"Thanks for everything. I have no complaints whatsoever."

— Neville

French Menu #7:

New Years Eve in Paris

Caviar Pie with Crackers
Wild Greens with Baked Goat Cheese
Salmon Escalopes with Lentils and Wild Rice
Glazed French Carrot Medley
Crème Brûlée

This menu cries for champagne and a special celebration, so why not New Year's Eve or any other special occasion that's worthy of this meal? If you do share this meal on New Year's Eve, you and your guests might reminisce over memorable times in the past year, discuss the ideas behind favorite quotes or prayers, or express goals for the new year. A New Year's prayer or meditation would be very special.

Caviar Pie with Crackers

Elegant alone, or as part of a cocktail buffet table.

Serves 10 to 12.

	1 large sweet onion, finely minced
6	hard-cooked large eggs, chopped fine
3 Tbs.	mayonnaise
2 Tbs.	butter, softened
	Salt and freshly ground black pepper to taste
8 oz.	cream cheese, softened
2/3 c.	sour cream
2 jars	caviar (2-oz. jars): 1 black, 1 red
1/4 c.	minced fresh Italian parsley

1. Allow minced onion to drain on paper towels for at least 30 minutes.
2. Butter bottom and sides of an 8-inch springform pan.
3. Combine finely chopped eggs with mayonnaise and butter, and season with salt and pepper. Spread evenly in bottom of springform pan. Top with finely minced onion.
4. Combine softened cream cheese with sour cream and carefully spoon over the onions.
5. Spread evenly with a wet knife. Chill several hours or overnight, covered tightly with plastic wrap.
6. Before serving, rinse caviar gently in a fine strainer, drain, and spoon one color of caviar on each half of the pie in a decorative pattern.
7. Sprinkle parsley around the edge of the circle of pie.
8. Run a damp knife around edge of pan and remove the sides of the springform mold. Transfer to a large serving platter and keep chilled until ready to serve. Serve with water biscuits or melba toast rounds.

"Happiness is having a sense of self — not a feeling of being perfect but of being good enough and knowing that you are in the process of growth, of being, of achieving levels of joy."
— Leo Buscaglia

Wild Greens with Baked Goat Cheese

Serves 6 to 8.

1 roll	French Chevre goat cheese, cut into 1/2-inch-thick slices
3/4 c.	extra-virgin olive oil
4 sprigs	fresh thyme
1 c.	fine, toasted bread crumbs
3 Tbs.	red wine vinegar
3/4 tsp.	salt
	Freshly ground black pepper to taste
8 c.	mixed fresh garden greens
1 c.	garlic croutons, homemade or packaged

1. Marinate the cheese overnight in some of the olive oil and all of the fresh thyme sprigs. Drain when ready to prepare the salad, and reserve the oil for another purpose. Remove the small leaves of thyme from the stems and chop finely, discarding the stems.
2. Mix chopped thyme and the bread crumbs together, and coat the drained cheese on both sides. Chill in refrigerator until ready to heat and serve.
3. Preheat oven to 400 degrees. Make a vinaigrette with the olive oil, red wine vinegar, salt, and pepper.
4. Bake breaded cheese rounds on a cookie sheet in oven for 6 minutes.
5. Toss the greens well with the some of the vinaigrette. Serve on individual salad plates: Place cheese on the side of the salad and scatter the croutons over the top. Serve immediately and pass the pepper mill.

There is no substitute for knowing what truly matters to you.

The Path of Least Resistance

Salmon Escalopes with Lentils and Wild Rice

Serves 6 to 8.

6 oz.	lentils
4 oz.	wild rice
1 tsp.	salt
2	bay leaves
2	medium onions, chopped
1	small yellow or red pepper, sliced thin
1 Tbs.	extra-virgin olive oil
1-1/2 Tbs.	grated fresh ginger
2 tsp.	cumin
2 c.	fish stock or canned clam juice
	Salt and freshly ground black pepper to taste
3 oz.	butter (measure on package)
16	salmon escalopes, 1-1/2 oz. each, or 8 small salmon fillets, about 3 oz. each
4 Tbs.	light soy sauce
2 Tbs.	fresh lemon juice
1-1/2 Tbs.	chopped fresh cilantro

Chopped fresh cilantro, for garnish

1. Soak lentils and rice together overnight in cold water. Many rice grains should split; this shortens the cooking time. Drain and return to a saucepan with plenty of water, 1 tsp. salt, and the bay leaves.
2. Bring to a boil; cook 20 minutes. Drain .
3. Gently sauté the onion and pepper in the oil for about 5 minutes, then stir in the ginger and cumin. Cook 1 to 2 minutes.
4. Add the lentils and rice, and the fish stock or clam juice. Season well with salt and pepper, and cook until most of the liquid has evaporated and the rice and lentils are tender. Remove bay leaves. Keep lentils and rice warm.
5. Heat butter in a sauté pan. When it is foaming, add the salmon escalopes or fillets, cooking on one side, till the fish feels firm. Season the fish with salt and pepper as you go, turning over and cooking for 1 minute longer, or just cooked through.
6. Sprinkle the soy sauce and lemon juice over the salmon.
7. Stir the fresh herbs into the lentils and rice, and spoon onto warm plates. Place fish on top and serve with a garnish of more herbs.

"Be gracious. Work with elegance."

— D.J.

Glazed French Carrot Medley

Serves 8.

1 lb.	French carrots, unpeeled
1-1/2 lbs.	parsnips
1 lb.	green beans
1/2 c.	butter
3 Tbs.	chopped fresh dill weed
	Salt and freshly ground black pepper to taste

1. Wash and scrape the carrots.
2. Peel the parsnips and cut into thick julienne strips about 2 inches long.
3. Wash and trim the beans.
4. Steam all vegetables separately, just till al dente.
5. Melt the butter and heat till golden brown. Add the dill and stir.
6. Place the vegetables side by side on a platter.
7. Pour the dill butter over the vegetables. Toss and season with salt and pepper. Serve immediately with the Salmon Escalopes, rice, and lentils.

"Love is stronger than hate."

— Anonymous

Crème Brûlée

This dessert is a favorite with many of us, even if it is rich, rich, rich! Once in a while it is important to treat yourself. There are many ways to fill your spirit, and sometimes a decadent dessert is just the answer. Serving fresh fruit like strawberries or orange slices on the side cuts the richness somewhat, if that's a problem. Besides, a fruit garnish does add some appealing color.

Serves 8.

2 c.	heavy cream
4	large egg yolks
1/2 c.	granulated sugar
1 Tbs.	vanilla extract

1. Preheat oven to 350 degrees. Heat cream over low heat until bubbles form around edge of pan.
2. Beat egg yolks and sugar together until thick and yellow, about 3 minutes.
3. Beating constantly, pour warm cream in a steady stream into egg yolks. Must not curdle the egg yolks!
4. Add vanilla and pour the custard into oven-proof custard cups (1/2-cup size).
5. Place custard cups in a baking pan that has from 1/2 to 1 inch of boiling water in the bottom of it. Bake for about 45 minutes or till set.
6. Remove custard cups from water bath, cool, and then refrigerate until chilled, about 2 hours.
7. Sprinkle each custard cup with some granulated sugar, about 1/2 to 1 tsp. Place the custards on a cookie sheet and place the cookie sheet on the top rack of the oven under the broiler. Broil the custards until sugar topping is medium brown. Be careful not to burn.
8. Refrigerate before serving.

My Way:

Baking the custards in a water bath keeps them nice and tender, so don't skip this step. It's worth it!

Chapter Five

The Mediterranean

Welcome to the cuisine of the countries on the Mediterranean Sea. There is a tangible awareness of spirit in the Mediterranean, expressed through art and architecture and the beauty of the sea itself. The people of this region built grand temples to their Gods, never dreaming that we would flock to visit them still, thousands of years later, from all over the world. We also "revisit" the foods and wines that have been prepared here over the centuries, which never seem to lose their allure. Somehow we are attracted to how these people lived and worked and sustained themselves. The connection is there and continues over time immemorial.

Mediterranean Menu #1:

A Spanish Dinner in Barcelona

Tortilla Española
Crostini and Roasted Red Pepper Spread
Gazpacho Andalusian
Paella Valencia
Baked Flan with Summer Fruits and Berries

Serve this dinner at the sea shore of your choice, vicariously envisioning the spirit, food, and culture of the Spanish people. Life is an adventure, so live it — explore new realms, even if it's just for a few hours at dinner. As you enjoy the splendid Paella Valencia, think of the fishermen on boats who go out to sea daily to bring in this variety of seafood, sometimes risking their lives to do so — and bless them for doing it.

Tortilla Española

Serves 10 to 12 as a first course.

4 to 6 Tbs.	extra-virgin olive oil
4 to 6 Tbs.	butter
8	medium onions, peeled, cut in half, and thinly sliced
	Salt and white pepper to taste
5	medium Idaho potatoes, peeled, halved, and sliced 1/8 inch thick
12	large eggs, lightly beaten
	Minced fresh Italian parsley
	Black olives

1. Heat the oil in a 10-inch skillet. Sprinkle the onion with salt and pepper, then sauté until soft. Remove the onions to a large bowl and set aside.
2. Add 2 to 3 Tbs. of oil and butter to the skillet, then add the potatoes. Sprinkle liberally with salt and pepper and cook, tossing occasionally with a rubber spatula, until golden and almost tender.
3. Place the potatoes and the lightly beaten eggs in the bowl with the cooked onions.
4. Add another 2 to 3 Tbs. more of the oil to the pan and heat. Pour in the egg and potato mixture and cook until it begins to set on the bottom. Lift the edges of the tortilla with a spatula, allowing the liquids to flow underneath. Cook over moderate heat until the omelet is firm and golden.
5. After the omelet becomes firm, cover it with a lid and continue to cook it till firmer and cooked through. Test with a knife — when inserted into the middle it should come out clean.
6. Cover the top of the skillet with a large serving platter and invert the skillet so that the tortilla is now on the platter. Garnish with parsley and black olives of your choice and serve immediately cut into wedges. Serve on individual small plates.

"Never is nothing happening."
— Jan Engels Smith

Crostini and Roasted Red Pepper Spread

Makes about 36 crostinis.

1	long, narrow loaf of Italian bread
	Olive oil spray
2 jars	roasted red peppers, drained (or roast your own) (7-oz. jars)
2 Tbs.	minced fresh Italian parsley
1 Tbs.	fresh lemon juice
1	medium clove garlic, crushed
2 Tbs.	extra-virgin olive oil
2 tsp.	capers, drained and rinsed
1/4 tsp.	salt

Whole, fresh basil leaves

1. Preheat oven to 350 degrees. Slice bread into 1/4-inch-thick slices. Place on a baking sheet and spray the top of the bread with olive oil. Turn the bread over and spray the other side. Bake until edges are lightly brown and centers are crisp, about 10 minutes.
2. Prepare spread: Arrange peppers on double layer of paper towels and let drain.
3. In the container of a food processor fitted with a metal blade, combine remaining ingredients. Process until capers and parsley are very finely chopped. Add drained peppers and process until peppers are coarsely chopped.
4. Check seasonings and adjust if necessary. Store spread in a covered container in refrigerator for up to 5 days. Allow mixture to come to room temperature before using. Makes 2 cups.
5. To serve, spread crostini thickly with the spread. Garnish with whole, fresh basil leaves.

Gazpacho Andalusian

This is a very easy-to-make version of the original that I feasted on many times while in Spain.

Serves 8 to 10.

1 can	whole Italian plum tomatoes, diced and in their liquid (1 lb., 11-oz.can)
1 can	tomato juice (46 oz.can)
1 c.	red wine vinegar
1/4 c.	extra-virgin olive oil
3 Tbs.	Worcestershire sauce
1 Tbs.	minced fresh oregano
2	cloves garlic, minced
1 tsp.	ground cumin
2	green bell peppers, chopped fine
1	medium cucumber, peeled and chopped fine
	Salt and freshly ground black pepper to taste
	Tabasco sauce to taste
1	avocado, peeled and sliced thin
1/2 c.	chopped Walla Walla or Vidalia onion
1 c.	garlic croutons, homemade or packaged

1. Combine first 10 ingredients. Mix well and season to taste with salt and pepper and Tabasco sauce. Chill for several hours.
2. Serve in chilled soup bowls garnished with avocado.
3. Pass chopped onion and croutons around the table.

"Consciously watch for inspiration."
— D.J.

Paella Valencia

I like to say that making paella is "easy but not simple." I have reinvented this recipe over the years with my favorite ingredients and proportions — believe me, your friends and family will love it, and you'll have fun preparing it. Paella is truly a feast for the eyes, and full of the variety of land and sea. Be sure to give thanks for all the abundance!

Serves 10 to 12.

3 Tbs.	extra-virgin olive oil
3 Tbs.	butter
1	whole chicken breast, boned, skinned, and cubed
2	chorizo sausages, removed from their casings
1	large onion, chopped
1	green pepper, chopped
2	cloves garlic, minced
2 c.	uncooked long-grain rice
2	bay leaves
1 tsp.	salt
	Freshly ground black pepper
1/4 tsp.	cayenne pepper
1/2 tsp.	ground coriander
1/2 tsp.	dried thyme
1 tsp.	dried oregano
1/2 tsp.	saffron
2 Tbs.	chopped fresh Italian parsley
1 c.	dry white wine
4 c	chicken stock. (1 qt.)
1 lb.	large, shelled, raw shrimp
1 lb.	fresh sea scallops
2 c.	fresh mushrooms, cleaned and sliced thick
1-1/2 lbs.	steamer clams, scrubbed
1-1/3 c.	frozen peas, thawed and drained
3/4 c.	pitted black olives, preferably Kalamata or Italian
1 can	artichoke hearts in water, drained and cut in half
2	large, ripe tomatoes, peeled, seeded, and cut into wedges
1/2 c.	pimento-stuffed green olives
2	lemons, cut into wedges, for garnish

1/4 c.   chopped fresh Italian parsley, for garnish

1. Heat 2 Tbs. oil and 2 Tbs. butter in a large sauté pan. Sauté chicken cubes and remove to a side dish.
2. Add sausage to pan and cook 5 minutes till crumbled and cooked through. Remove from pan and add to reserved chicken.
3. Add 2 Tbs. oil and 1 Tbs. butter to the pan. Sauté onions, green pepper, and garlic till soft.
4. Add rice and stir to coat grains with oil and butter.
5. Return chicken and sausage to the pan. Add the bay leaves.
6. In another pan, heat the stock and season it with the salt, pepper, cayenne, coriander, thyme, oregano, saffron, and 2 Tbs. chopped parsley.
7. Pour white wine into rice mixture, stir, and cook till liquid has almost evaporated.
8. Pour hot stock into rice mixture and bring to a boil. Turn down to a simmer and cover the pan. Simmer gently on top of stove for approximately 35 minutes or until all of the stock is absorbed.
9. Add the tomatoes and their juice. Simmer lightly till most of the juice is absorbed.
10. About 15 minutes before paella is done, sauté the shrimp, scallops, and the mushrooms individually in a small amount of olive oil and butter. Reserve.
11. Add the cleaned clams, open side up, to the paella. Cover and steam for 3 minutes.
12. Add everything else to the paella and heat through, stirring with a rubber spatula so as not to break up any of the ingredients. Note: Do not eat any of the clams that don't open; discard them. (Even if you are not a clam lover, you MUST include them as the clam shells add a lot to the look, feel, and taste of this dish.)
13. When everything is hot, decorate with lemon wedges and chopped parsley. I like to serve this right in the cooking pan, in the center of the table, family style, letting everyone serve themselves with a big spoon. Serve with hot, hearty crusty bread and butter or individual olive oil dipping bowls — perhaps with a little minced oregano and garlic floating in them. Enjoy!

Baked Flan with Summer Fruits and Berries

Flan must be made at least 6 hours before serving so that it has enough time to chill thoroughly. It may be prepared up to 2 days in advance and stored in the refrigerator, loosely covered with plastic wrap. Do not freeze. Flavored, mixed fruit make up the second part of this recipe.

Serves 8 to 10.

Flan:

One 6- to 8-cup mold

1-3/4 c.	sugar
4	whole large eggs
4	large egg yolks
2	cans evaporated milk (13-oz. cans)
2-1/2 tsp.	vanilla extract
1/4 c.	brandy or rum (to flame the custard at table, optional)

1. Preheat oven to 350 degrees. In a heavy-bottomed saucepan, heat 1 c. of the sugar over medium-high heat. Stir constantly until the sugar melts completely and turns a golden brown. Be careful not to touch the caramel with your hands as it is very hot.
2. Pour the caramel into the mold, then rotate the mold to coat the sides with the caramel. Set aside to cool while making the custard. The caramel will harden inside the mold, but will become liquid again during the baking.
3. Make the custard: Beat the eggs and extra yolks together in a blender or a large mixing bowl.
4. Add the milk, the remaining 1/4 cup of sugar, and the vanilla, and blend or stir for 20 to 30 seconds.
5. Pour this mixture into the caramel-coated mold, cover, and set it in a larger pan containing an inch or more of hot water.
6. Bake the custard in its water bath for 1 hour and 15 minutes, or longer, until a knife inserted into the center comes out clean. You may refrigerate the flan until ready to turn it out, or let it cool for 10 to 15 minutes and then invert it carefully onto a serving plate with a rim, to catch the liquid caramel. Chill for several hours.

"Begin at once
To live and count each
day
As a separate life."
— Anonymous

7. At serving time, heat the brandy or rum, ignite it, and pour over the flan. When the flame has died, cut the flan into wedges, and serve with the liquor-soaked fruit.

Fruit (all or some of these fruits are possibilities):

1 c.	fresh pineapple, cubed
1 c.	banana, peeled and cut into 1/2-inch-thick slices
1 c.	sliced nectarine
1 c.	raspberries or other berries
1/2 c.	orange liqueur
1 Tbs.	rum or brandy
1/4 c.	toasted coconut

1. Mix all of the fruit except the berries in a medium-sized bowl.
2. Add the alcohol and stir with a rubber spatula. Let sit at room temperature for one hour.
3. Place the fruit mixture in a serving bowl and sprinkle the berries over it. You may place some of the mixed fruit atop the unmolded flan. Sprinkle the toasted coconut over all and serve immediately.

Mediterranean Dinner #2:

At the Pier in Marseille

Fritto Misto with Sauce Verte
Bouillabaisse
Herbed Garlic Bread
Brie à la Vierge
Dacquoise with Coffee Butter Cream

Here's another menu that speaks of the sea. Friends and family will love this seafood stew, and an opportunity to reminisce about your own fishing trips or visits to the Mediterranean, whether fishing, sightseeing, or touring the bustling harbor of Marseille. Pull out the photographs of fish caught, and remember those that got away. Memories associated with food offer a wonderful way to share loving adventures.

Fritto Misto with Sauce Verte

This first course is especially good in the summertime with the abundance of vegetables at very reasonable prices. My favorite are zucchini blossoms, which can be purchased in specialties stores or summer farmer's markets. The sauce verte is good with raw vegetables as well.

Make and serve to as many as you like.

Sauce Verte:

1 c.	loosely packed fresh spinach leaves
3 sprigs	fresh Italian parsley
1/4 c.	watercress, leaves only
2 Tbs.	fresh lemon juice
2 Tbs.	green onions
1/4 tsp.	dry mustard
1 tsp.	dried basil or tarragon
2	anchovy fillets, or 2-1/2 Tbs. anchovy paste (comes in a tube)
1 c.	mayonnaise
	Dash Tabasco sauce
2 Tbs.	capers, rinsed and drained
	Salt and freshly ground black pepper to taste

1. Remove stems from spinach. Wash and dry thoroughly.
2. Place spinach and all other ingredients except capers in blender or food processor, and process for 10 to 15 seconds.
3. Pour into a container and fold in the capers. Taste for seasoning, and add salt and pepper to taste. Refrigerate till chilled.

Vegetable Ideas:

Artichoke hearts
Asparagus
Broccoli
Carrots
Cauliflower
Green or yellow beans
Italian parsley
Mushrooms
Red, green, yellow peppers
Zucchini
Zucchini blossoms.

Batter:

1 c.	water
2/3 c.	all-purpose flour

3 to 4 c.   canola oil, for frying

1. Prepare the vegetables and have them dried and ready on a platter, all in bite-size chunks, except leave the zucchini blossoms and the mushrooms whole. The zucchini blossoms should be washed and dried very gently in one whole piece.
2. Prepare another platter lined with paper towels. Keep extra paper towels handy.
3. Place the oil in a deep saucepan like a Dutch oven or deep fryer, and heat to hot but not burning. Test the oil with one vegetable piece. The oil should sizzle and quickly cook the piece golden brown, within a minute or so. If the oil does not sizzle, then it's not hot enough. On the other hand, if it's so hot that the vegetables are almost burning, then turn down the heat a little. This is the only tricky part with fritto misto — controlling the heat if the oil. Raise and lower the temperature as needed, and remember, at any time you can just take the pan off the heat for a minute.
4. For the batter, mix flour and water to make a thin paste.
5. Dip the vegetables in batter and gently drop into the hot oil. Be very careful not to burn yourself with the hot oil.
6. Cook till golden brown, 30 to 60 seconds or so, until lightly golden brown. Drain on paper towels.
7. Place the drained, hot vegetables on a serving tray lined with a clean white napkin or kitchen towel and serve immediately with the sauce verte and salt and pepper. Make enough for each person to have 5 to 6 pieces (or more if you have hungry guests).

"When thinking of having a dinner party, 'feel the fear and then do it anyway.' Confront your culinary demons!"

— D.J.

Bouillabaisse

Complete this recipe up to the end of step 2 ahead of time. Then refrigerate it, or freeze the sauce until fresh seafood is in season. When you go to the beach for a weekend, take the frozen sauce along and buy fresh seafood at the beach. All you have to do is heat the sauce and slowly add the fresh seafood for a very easy, quick, delicious beach dinner that everyone will enjoy.

Serves 6.

2 Tbs.	butter
2 Tbs.	extra-virgin olive oil
1	carrot, chopped
1/2 c.	minced onion
1	large clove garlic, minced
1-1/4 c.	canned tomatoes, with their liquid
2 Tbs.	tomato paste
4 c. (1 qt.)	chicken stock
1 qt.	bottled clam juice
1 tsp.	dry basil, or 1 Tbs. fresh
3 Tbs.	minced fresh Italian parsley
2 strips	orange zest, (3-inch)
1-1/2 lbs.	halibut
1-1/2 lbs.	large, shelled, raw shrimp
1-1/2 lbs.	sea scallops
1-1/2 lbs.	fresh clams, cleaned and scrubbed
1/2 c.	white wine
2 tsp.	salt
1/8 tsp.	white pepper

NOTE: You may add or substitute any other seafood as well. These are my favorites. Other options: crab, red snapper, salmon, squid, octopus.

1. Sauté carrot, onion, and garlic in butter and oil till tender, 10 to 15 minutes.
2. Add tomatoes, tomato paste, stock, clam juice, herbs, and orange zest; simmer 15 minutes.
3. Cut fish into manageable chunks and gradually add to stew. Cook 4 to 5 minutes. Then add whole shrimp, scallops, and clams last, as they need the least cooking — you don't want to overcook them because they'll be tough. Discard any clams that do not open after cooked.
4. Add the white wine and correct seasoning. Heat through and serve with crusty French garlic bread.

"Give until it hurts."
— Mother Teresa

Herbed Garlic Bread

Serves 8 to 10.

1	good-quality loaf French bread
1/2 c.	butter, softened
1 clove	garlic, crushed
1/3 c.	grated Parmesan cheese
1/4 c.	minced fresh Italian parsley

1. Cut bread lengthwise into two pieces.
2. Mix the butter and garlic, and spread on the sliced part of the bread.
3. Sprinkle the cheese and the parsley over the buttered bread.
4. Place on cookie sheet and broil 6 inches from broiler, 2 to 3 minutes or just till lightly golden and bubbling.

"ALWAYS leave people their dignity."

— D.J.

Brie à la Vierge

You could stop here and have this be the dessert if you wish. Very nice ending to a memorable meal. The French always serve cheese before a dessert so I'm offering you both.

Serves 6 to 8.

1 round	Brie cheese (5- to 6-inch)
6 Tbs.	flour
2	large eggs, beaten with 2 to 3 Tbs. milk
1-1/2 c.	lightly toasted bread crumbs
	Salt to taste
	Butter, for sautéing
	Fruit slices

1. Cut the wheel of Brie in half horizontally to form 2 wheels.
2. Dredge each of the rounds: first in the flour, then in the beaten eggs, then in the bread crumbs and salt.
3. Repeat step two. The crust should be quite thick.
4. Melt some butter in a skillet and sauté the cheese till golden brown and crisp on both sides.
5. Serve at once with tart, sliced apples, grapes and/or pears, and good French baguette.

Dacquoise with Coffee Butter Cream

This dessert is more uptown Paris, but it is a rich way to end this healthy meal. I like the combination of the unassuming Bouillabaisse and the elegant Dacquoise together in the same meal.

Serves 12.

Dacquoise:

5	large egg whites (reserve yolks for Coffee Butter Cream, below)
1/8 tsp.	cream of tartar
1-1/4 c.	sugar
1 c.	ground, blanched almonds
1/2 c.	zwieback crumbs
2 Tbs.	sifted flour
2 Tbs.	sifted cornstarch
1 tsp.	vanilla extract

1. Beat egg whites and cream of tartar till frothy. Gradually add 3/4 c. sugar while beating, and continue beating till stiff.
2. Fold in the remaining sugar, almonds, zwieback, flour, cornstarch, and vanilla.
3. Cut three 8-inch circles of waxed paper. Place on baking sheets.
4. Spoon meringue onto circles and smooth with a knife.
5. Bake for 45 to 60 minutes. Cool to room temperature.

Coffee Butter Cream:

1 c.	sugar
1/3 c.	water
1/8 tsp.	cream of tartar
5	large egg yolks
1 c.	butter, softened
2 Tbs.	instant coffee
2 Tbs.	Grand Marnier
	Shaved chocolate
1 c.	heavy cream, whipped stiff with 2 Tbs. powdered sugar and 1 tsp. vanilla extract

1. Combine sugar, water, and cream of tartar in saucepan. Stir over low heat until dissolved. Raise heat and boil till

it reaches 240 degrees on a candy thermometer (soft ball stage.)

2. While this cooks, beat the egg yolks till they become pale yellow and double in volume.

3. Pour the sugar syrup very slowly into egg yolks, beating constantly.

4. Set aside to cool. When cool, beat in softened butter bit by bit.

5. Stir in instant coffee and Grand Marnier to taste.

6. Spread butter cream on the meringue, garnish the top with shaved chocolate, and pipe sweetened whipped cream around the edges. Chill until ready to serve, or freeze whole or in pieces, wrapped very tightly.

Mediterranean Menu #3:

A Greek Taverna Dinner

Virginia's Hummus
Greek Taverna Salad with Oregano Dressing
Stuffed Grape Leaves
Chicken in Phyllo
Rice à la Grecque
Steamed Ginger Puddings and Butterscotch Sauce

My favorite places to eat in Greece are the tavernas. They are alive with spirit, from the sincere hospitality of the taverna owners to the grape arbors that hang over the patios to shield the guests from the hot Greek sun. Charm, charm, charm all the way! Taste this menu, and share in that spirit.

Virginia's Hummus

Serves 8 to 10 as an appetizer.

1/3 c.	minced onion
3	cloves garlic, minced
1 Tbs.	extra-virgin olive oil
1 tsp.	sesame seed oil
1 c.	canned garbanzo beans, drained and rinsed
1/4 c.	nonfat sour cream
1/4 c.	fresh lemon juice
1 tsp.	salt
2 Tbs.	tahini (sesame paste)
	Salt and freshly ground black pepper to taste
6 to 8	whole pita breads

1. Sauté onion and garlic in 1 Tbs. olive oil until soft but not brown.
2. Add remaining ingredients to food processor with the onions and garlic.
3. Blend all till smooth. Add salt and pepper to taste.
4. Serve with pieces of toasted pita bread which has been separated and cut in quarters, sprayed with oil and broiled till golden brown.

"My Spirit brings me peace of heart, mind, and body."

— Anonymous

Greek Taverna Salad with Oregano Dressing

In Greece, this salad is brought to the table on a plate or platter and set in the middle of the table for everyone to share with hearty Greek bread. Simple and delicious.

Serves 4 to 6.

1	large cucumber
2	ripe tomatoes
1	red or Walla Walla onion
1	green pepper
1	yellow pepper
1 c.	Kalamata olives
1 lb.	imported Greek goat cheese

Dressing:

6 Tbs.	extra-virgin olive oil
2 Tbs.	white wine vinegar
1/2 tsp.	salt
1 tsp.	dried oregano
	Freshly ground black pepper to taste

1. Cut the vegetables into large chunks and place in a bowl with the olives.
2. Cut the goat cheese into 1-inch cubes and add to the vegetables.
3. Mix all of the dressing ingredients in a screw-top jar and toss with the vegetables and cheese.
4. Pour into a shallow bowl or onto a serving platter and serve immediately with hearty bread.

"Ask and you shall receive
Search and you shall find
Knock and the door shall be open unto to you."
— The Bible

Stuffed Grape Leaves

These are really not difficult to make but are a little time-consuming. If you don't want to fix your own, buy them from your local deli.

Serves 8 to 10.

20	large grape leaves, or dolmathes (about half a jar; domestic leaves are more tender)
1	onion, diced
2 Tbs.	minced fresh Italian parsley
2 Tbs.	extra-virgin olive oil
1 lb.	ground lamb or beef
1 c.	tomato sauce
2 tsp.	dried mint, or 3 Tbs. chopped fresh
3/4 tsp.	cinnamon
1/4 tsp.	grated fresh nutmeg
1	clove garlic, minced
1 tsp.	fresh lemon juice
1	bay leaf
1 c.	cooked long-grain rice
1-1/4 c.	beef stock

1. Preheat oven to 350 degrees. Remove grape leaves from jar, pat dry, and lay out on a board, vein side up, and cut off the stem.
2. Heat the oil in a sauté pan and sauté the onion and minced garlic; cook until tender.
3. Mix in a bowl: the ground meat, rice, onion, garlic, mint, cinnamon, nutmeg, and half of the tomato sauce. Mix well.
4. Place 1 heaping Tbs. of filling onto each grape leaf and roll up, tucking in the ends. Place in a baking pan, seam side down.
5. Mix together: the other half of the tomato sauce, the beef stock, lemon juice, and bay leaf.
6. Pour above mixture over the stuffed grape leaves. Use about 3 to 4 extra grape leaves from the jar to cover the stuffed grape leaves. This prevents them from drying out.
7. Bake, covered, for 45 minutes. Serve immediately.

Chicken in Phyllo

This dish is not for the faint of heart to prepare, but think of it this way: it's a great and delicious way to learn how to deal with Greek pastry.

Serves 4 to 6.

2 Tbs.	chopped onion
1	clove garlic , crushed
4 Tbs.	butter, divided
1 c.	sliced mushrooms, divided
3/4 c.	heavy cream
	Salt and freshly ground black pepper to taste
4	boned and skinned chicken breasts halves
5 to 6 sheets	phyllo dough, thawed (purchase prepared phyllo in the frozen foods section of your supermarket)
1/2 c.	melted butter
1	large egg
1 tsp.	water

1. Preheat oven to 425 degrees. Sauté onion and garlic in 2 Tbs. butter for one minute. Add 1/3 c. mushrooms and sauté an additional 3 minutes.
2. Place in blender or food processor with 1/2 c. cream, and purée. Season to taste with salt and pepper, and set aside.
3. Flatten chicken breasts slightly and slice into 1-inch strips. In a large frying pan, sauté the chicken in remaining 2 Tbs. butter until brown. Remove from pan and set aside.
4. Sauté remaining 2/3 c. mushrooms in same pan for 2 minutes. Turn heat to low.
5. Return chicken to pan along with mushroom purée. Stir to combine well. If necessary, stir in additional cream, a little at a time. There should be just enough sauce to coat chicken and mushrooms.
6. Have 6 thawed sheets of phyllo ready under a damp cloth.
7. Place first sheet on counter and brush well with melted butter. Place second sheet on top and brush it with butter. Repeat until all the phyllo is used up. With the last sheet, do not brush the entire surface with butter — only a border around the outside edges.

"We are all works in progress, and still learning! We are works of love created by God."

— D.J.

8. Arrange chicken mixture lengthwise over a third of the pastry, leaving a 2-inch border around outside edges.
9. Fold in bottom edge of pastry, then sides. Carefully roll up, jelly-roll fashion. Place on ungreased baking sheet, seam side down.
10. Beat egg and water together and brush on pastry to glaze. Bake for 12 to 15 minutes, until pastry is crisp. Slice into 2-inch pieces and serve immediately.

Rice à la Grecque

Serves 8 to 10.

1 c.	uncooked long-grain rice
2-1/4 c.	chicken stock
1 tsp.	marjoram
1 tsp.	salt
3 Tbs.	butter, cut into small pieces

Vegetables:

2 Tbs.	butter or oil
1/4 c.	pine nuts
1	onion, diced fine
1	clove garlic , minced
1/4 lb.	mushrooms, wiped clean and sliced thick
1/2	green pepper, chopped
4	romaine lettuce leaves, shredded
2	peeled tomatoes, chopped
1/2 c.	frozen green peas, thawed and drained
4 Tbs.	raisins

1. Preheat oven to 350 degrees. Butter a casserole dish. Mix rice, stock, marjoram, and butter pieces, and place in the casserole dish.

2. Bake uncovered 45 minutes. Stir and bake for 10 to 15 minutes more, still uncovered. The rice will be moist and fluffy when done.

3. Heat 2 Tbs. of the butter or oil and sauté nuts till golden. Remove to a dish.

4. Add the onions and garlic to pan and sauté till tender. Add mushrooms and cook 2 minutes.

5. Toss in green pepper, lettuce, tomatoes, peas, and raisins. Cook very quickly and toss all this into the rice. Garnish with pine nuts and serve immediately.

Steamed Ginger Puddings and Butterscotch Sauce

This wonderful pudding also fits as a "comfort food."

Serves 12.

1/3 c.	ginger cake crumbs (purchase ginger cake from a bakery or bake your own)
1/3 c.	fresh bread crumbs
2 tsp.	cocoa
2 tsp.	ground ginger
2 tsp.	ground cinnamon
1/4 c.	ground almonds
1 Tbs.	flour
8 Tbs.	ginger wine, from ginger soaked in sherry (see "My Way," following Tom Yum Shrimp Soup in the Asian section of this book)
5	large eggs, separated
	Pinch of salt
1/2 c.	butter
1/4 c.	brown sugar
1/2 c.	granulated sugar

Butterscotch Sauce:

1 c.	heavy cream
1-1/4 c.	sugar
2/3 c.	water

Nonfat frozen yogurt

1. Preheat oven to 375 degrees. Prepare the pudding: In a large bowl mix together the ginger cake crumbs, bread crumbs, cocoa, ground ginger, and cinnamon. Add the ground almonds and flour. Mix well and set aside.
2. In a bowl, beat egg yolks till thick and lemon-colored. Add to the dry mixture and blend in well.
3. In another bowl, beat egg whites with a pinch of salt until they reach soft peaks.
4. Gradually add the sugar, and continue beating until the whites reach firm peaks. Gently fold the egg whites into the crumb and egg yolk mixture, and stir until well blended.

5. Butter and sugar 12 timbale molds or custard cups and pour in the mixture. Place molds in a baking dish with boiling water to reach 1/3 of the way up the individual molds. Bake 15 to 20 minutes or until puddings are firm.

6. Make the butterscotch sauce: Bring cream to a boil and remove from the heat.

7. In a separate sauté pan, cook the sugar with the water and boil together until it is a rich, golden brown.

8. Away from the stove, carefully pour the caramel into the cream, taking care not to burn your fingers as the cream is very hot and bubbly.

9. Whisk thoroughly to blend, return to the stove, and cook until the butterscotch is smooth.

10. Unmold the puddings onto individual serving plates, pour the butterscotch sauce over and around, and serve with a scoop of frozen yogurt, slightly softened, on the side.

"Do not pray for anything! Pray for the attainment of the realization of God, and stop there."
— Joel Goldsmith

Mediterranean Menu #4:

Flavors from the Middle East

Spicy Chicken Wings
Couscous Salad
Braised Lamb Shanks and Artichoke Hearts in Lemon Sauce
Puréed Garlic Potatoes with Pine Nuts
Persian Pancakes

There is great variety in the exotic flavors indigenous to this part of the world. Some dishes use lots of spices to flavor bland foods, like the staples of rice and couscous, while others are simply grilled or braised and enhanced with lots of lemon. Whether simple or complex, these dishes reflect the convergence of many cultures from surrounding regions. The creative spirit flows from one country and culture to another through their ways of preparing food and their customs of partaking of these dishes. At the end of your meal, if you're feeling dramatic, have everyone read a paragraph or two from The Arabian Nights to invoke the spirit of the Middle East.

Spicy Chicken Wings

Serves 10 to 12 as an appetizer.

4 lbs.	chicken wings (about 20 to 24, tips cut off)
4	cloves garlic
2	shallots
1-1/2 tsp.	salt
1 Tbs.	Chinese five-spice powder
2 tsp.	paprika
1 tsp.	dried, crumbled rosemary
1/2 tsp.	cayenne, or to taste
2 Tbs.	canola oil

Sauce:

1/3 c.	natural-style peanut butter
1/4 c.	canned coconut milk, well stirred
2	cloves garlic, chopped
1/4 c.	water
1/4 c.	chopped red bell pepper
1/4 tsp.	red pepper flakes, or to taste
1 tsp.	soy sauce

Fresh cilantro sprigs

1. Prepare the chicken wings and place in a large bowl or container. In small bowl, mince the garlic and the shallots, and blend into a paste. Add the salt and all the seasonings. Add the oil. Blend all well and pour over the chicken wings. Coat well; cover and chill 4 hours or overnight.
2. Preheat oven to 425 degrees. Arrange the chicken wings, skin sides up, on the rack of a large, foil-lined broiler pan. Bake 25 to 30 minutes or until golden brown. May be baked 1 day in advance, covered, and then reheated.
3. Make the sauce: In food processor bowl, blend together all sauce ingredients till smooth. Season with salt to taste.
4. Transfer to a serving bowl, set on a platter, and arrange the chicken wings around the bowl. Garnish with the fresh cilantro.

"The closer we become to God, the more Spirit-like we become."

— D.J.

Couscous Salad

Simple, easy, healthy, and delicious. Great to take on a picnic or potluck, too.

Serves 6.

6 c.	chicken stock or water
1 c.	couscous
2	cloves garlic, minced
1/4 c.	extra-virgin olive oil, plus more for sautéing garlic
1/2 c.	white wine vinegar
	Salt and freshly ground black pepper to taste
1 can	garbanzo beans, drained and rinsed
1 c.	currants
1 c.	pine nuts
1	large cucumber, peeled, seeded, and chopped fine
2	green peppers, cored, seeded, and chopped fine
1	red onion, peeled and chopped fine
1/2 c.	chopped green onions
1/2 c.	chopped fresh Italian parsley
	Fresh lemon juice, optional

Lettuce leaves
Lemon zest strips

Thought is creative.
Fear attracts like energy.
Love is all there is.
                    Anonymous

1. In a large pot, bring stock or water to a boil. Slowly stir in the couscous. Turn off heat and let sit for 5 minutes, then fluff gently with a fork.
2. Sauté the garlic cloves in a small amount of olive oil and add them to the couscous.
3. Turn couscous out into a large bowl. Sprinkle the quarter-cup of olive oil and the vinegar over all, and season with salt and pepper to taste.
4. Add garbonzo beans and fluff couscous again with a fork. Allow couscous to cool.
5. When cool, add remaining ingredients and mix well. Taste and correct seasonings. Add lemon juice if desired.
6. Place washed and dried lettuce leaves on a large platter or individual salad plates and mound the salad on the lettuce leaves. Top with a sliver of lemon zest and serve.

Braised Lamb Shanks and Artichokes Heart in Lemon Sauce

These lamb shanks taste especially great when it's cold, dark, and rainy — they're hearty and comforting. The lemon-flavored sauce is great on mashed potatoes.

Serves 8.

8	meaty lamb shanks, uncracked
4 Tbs.	fresh lemon juice, divided
	Salt and freshly ground black pepper to taste
4 Tbs.	extra-virgin olive oil
2	cloves garlic, minced
1 tsp.	dried oregano
2	onions, quartered
2 c.	chicken stock
2 cans	artichoke hearts in water, drained and cut in half
2 Tbs.	cornstarch
1/2 c.	water

1. Preheat oven to 300 degrees. Rub the lamb shanks with 2 Tbs. lemon juice and salt and pepper to taste.
2. In a skillet sauté the shanks in the olive oil, adding a little oil at a time.
3. Turn the shanks until they are evenly browned on all sides.
4. Transfer the shanks and oil to a casserole and sprinkle the meat with remaining lemon juice, garlic, and oregano. Add the onion and bake the casserole, covered, for 2-1/2 hours.
5. Add 2 c. chicken stock and the artichoke hearts. Raise the oven heat to 350 degrees and bake the casserole, covered, another 30 minutes.
6. Transfer lamb and artichokes to a hot serving platter and keep warm. Thicken the juices in the casserole with 2 Tbs. cornstarch blended with the half-cup of water, and serve the sauce separately over the lamb and Puréed Garlic Potatoes with Pine Nuts.

"Trust in your feelings They are the voices of your soul."
— Walt Rincler

Puréed Garlic Potatoes with Pine Nuts

Serves 6 to 8.

3 Tbs.	extra-virgin olive oil
3	onions, peeled and sliced thin
	Salt and freshly ground black pepper to taste

2 lbs.	potatoes
5 Tbs.	butter
1/3 c.	milk (or more)
	Salt and white pepper to taste

3 Tbs.	toasted pine nuts

1. Heat oil in a sauté pan and fry the onion over medium to high heat, tossing frequently, until onions are cooked and some are crisp and golden. Add salt and pepper to taste.
2. Cook the peeled and quartered potatoes in boiling, salted water until tender, then drain.
3. Add the butter, some milk, salt, and white pepper to taste. Crush with a potato masher until potatoes are light and fluffy, adding more milk, salt, and pepper as required.
4. Serve the potatoes covered with the onions and sprinkle with toasted pine nuts.
5. Pass the sauce and serve it over the lamb shanks and the potatoes.

Persian Pancakes

This 3-part dessert starts with crêpelike pancakes.

Serves 6 to 8.

A. Make the pancakes.

Pancake Batter:

1 c.	flour
1 tsp.	baking powder
1-1/2 c.	milk
2	large eggs
1 tsp.	melted butter

1. Mix the baking powder with the flour. Add the milk and beat with a wire whisk.
2. Add eggs and butter until the mixture forms a smooth paste. Batter should be thinner than hotcake batter.
3. Cook the pancakes in a crêpe pan and stack on a plate. Keep warm.

B. Make the filling, then fill and bake the pancakes.

Filling:

2 c.	cottage cheese
1 c.	raisins
1/2 c.	brown sugar
2 tsp.	ground cinnamon

1. Preheat oven to 350 degrees. Purée the cottage cheese in food processor. Remove it to a bowl and stir in the rest of the ingredients.
2. Place 2 Tbs. filling on each pancake and roll up.
3. Place in a baking pan, seam side down and bake for 10 minutes, covered.

"Courage is grace under pressure."

C. Make the sauce and assemble the dessert.

Sauce:

2 c.	apple cider
1 to 2 Tbs.	cornstarch
3 Tbs.	Apple Jack brandy
2	sliced apples, sautéed in 1 Tbs. butter and 1 Tbs. sugar
1 qt.	good-quality vanilla ice cream

1. Dissolve the cornstarch in half the apple cider.
2. Heat the other half and when it starts to boil, add the juice with the cornstarch, stirring with a wire whisk to prevent lumping. Cook over low heat 2 to 3 minutes, then add the brandy and the cooked apples.
3. To assemble: Place two of the filled pancakes on each individual plate with a scoop of vanilla ice cream on the side. Spoon some of the sauce with apples over the dessert and serve immediately.

Chapter Six

Asia

Along with Italian food, Asian cuisine has been all the rage in the nineties. What a combination! I wonder what new food experiences the coming years will bring. We in the U.S. have embraced Asian culture, from yoga, meditation, and the teachings of Asian mystics and teachers to Asian foods, herbs, spices, and ways of living. Our homes and furnishings have become more simple and uncluttered. We have "borrowed" the clean pastels and white and black combinations, all the way down to our dishes and serving pieces. And Feng Shui, the Chinese art of placement, is being taught everywhere. There are many consultants as well as books to introduce you to the art of Feng Shui.

Asian dishes are healthy and delicious. Nothing quite suffices when I'm in the mood for a certain Thai dish, or Chinese fried rice and deep-fried shrimp with hot mustard. These menus and recipes have come from across Asia and around the world, and I have added my own twists to appeal to my taste buds. I do hope you enjoy them.

Asian Menu #1:

A Thai Dinner

Thai Spring Rolls and Sauce
Tom Yum Shrimp Soup
Evil Jungle Prince with Chicken and Vegetables
Steamed Jasmine Rice
Pumpkin Crème Brûlée

When I lived in Hawaii I frequented a Thai restaurant called Keo's that was my favorite restaurant anywhere. Not only was the food to die for, the atmosphere was lovely and exotic, with huge bouquets of orchids sitting on high pedestals and lit with spotlights. The place was filled with giant banana palms, golden Buddhas, and large, beautiful oil paintings of Thai scenes hung on the walls. It was truly a feast for the body, mind, and spirit. Though it was very popular, I am told that it's no longer in business, which is truly a tragedy.

These spring rolls are adapted from Keo's, along with the Evil Jungle Prince, which has a wonderful coconut sauce that is always a favorite. I should mention here that I am not fond of most Asian desserts, so I have adapted my own to each of these meals, blending desserts that work with the food but are much more elegant and flavorful than true Asian desserts — at least in my opinion. May the Asian Gods forgive me.

Thai Spring Rolls and Sauce

I know you'll think this recipe looks like too much work, but these spring rolls are worth the effort because the combination of flavors is ambrosial. This is a great dish to get everyone in on the preparations (or to make way ahead of time by yourself). The first few rolls can look pretty amateurish, but soon everyone gets the hang of it and concentrates on making the best and tightest rolls. I always tease my students who make the misshapen first ones, telling them that they'll have to eat those themselves. It's really fun when you share this cooking "experience."

Makes about 4 dozen spring rolls.

Spring Roll Sauce:

1/4 c.	sugar
1/2 c.	water
1/2 c.	red wine vinegar
1 to 2 tsp.	fish sauce or 1/2 tsp. salt
2 to 3	ground fresh red chile peppers, or 1/4 tsp. red pepper flakes
1/2	carrot, shredded
1/4 c.	coarsely chopped roasted, salted peanuts

1. In a small saucepan combine sugar and water; bring to a boil.
2. Reduce and simmer for about 10 minutes or till sugar is dissolved.
3. Remove from heat. Stir in red wine vinegar, fish sauce, and red chile.
4. Pour sauce into serving bowl. Chill, then top with carrots and sprinkle with peanuts before serving. Makes 1 cup sauce.

1/4 lb.	fresh ground pork
1/4 lb.	raw, shelled shrimp, chopped
10	dried Chinese black mushrooms
1/2 c.	jelly noodles (a kind of transparent vermicelli found in Oriental markets)
1	medium onion, chopped fine
1	carrot, shredded
1/4 lb.	bean sprouts, rinsed and drained
1/2 tsp.	freshly ground black pepper

2 tsp.	fish sauce (buy the best quality you can)
1 Tbs.	soy sauce
1 tsp.	sugar
1 bowl	lukewarm water
8	quartered rice papers (purchase them in the refrigerator or freezer section of a Chinese market)
6 c.	canola oil for deep frying
48	small lettuce leaves
1 bunch	fresh mint
1	English cucumber, thinly sliced with skin left on
1 recipe	Spring Roll Sauce
1/2 c.	chopped roasted, salted peanuts

1. Combine pork and shrimp in a bowl and set aside.
2. Soak mushrooms in water for 20 minutes. Then remove stems by cutting them off with a sharp knife or scissors; discard. Chop the caps and reserve.
3. Soak jelly noodles in warm water for 20 minutes. Then cut into 1-inch lengths.
4. To pork mixture add mushrooms, jelly noodles, onion, carrot, bean sprouts, black pepper, and the soy and fish sauces; mix well. Set aside for 15 minutes to allow flavors to blend.
5. Dilute the sugar in the bowl of lukewarm water. Dip one rice paper at a time in the lukewarm water gently to soften it. Place it on a clean work surface.
6. Place 2 tsp. of filling near the edge of the rice paper, then fold rice paper over the filling. Fold the right side over to enclose filling, then fold over the left side.
7. Continue to roll, then seal. Place the rolls on a large platter and cover them with a dampened tea towel.
8. Heat oil for deep-frying to 375 degrees on a thermometer. Deep-fry a few rolls at a time until crisp and golden brown, about 1 to 2 minutes. This goes really fast, so be prepared with your slotted spoon to remove them, and a tray lined in paper towels to drain them on. Adjust the heat if the oil is too hot or not hot enough. If too hot, the rolls will come apart; if not hot enough, the rolls will just sit there and absorb too much oil. When they rise to the top and are also golden brown, they're done.
9. Keep them warm in a low oven, but don't cover them or

they'll lose their crispness.

10.   Fix a platter with the lettuce leaves, mint, and cucumber slices on it and place on the table. Serve the spring rolls as soon as possible along with the spring roll sauce. The process is: Place a lettuce leaf on your plate, then a spring roll on top of that; next some mint and cucumber slices, then a spoonful of the sauce, and finally a scattering of chopped peanuts. Roll it all up, tucking in the ends, and enjoy!

Tom Yum Shrimp Soup

This authentic soup calls for Galongo ginger from Thailand. It's different from the regular, edible Chinese ginger sold in supermarkets. Galongo's flavor is more intense, but it is too tough to eat. You'll find Galongo ginger and many of the other ingredients in your local Asian market.

Serves 6 to 8.

2 Tbs.	canola oil
1/2 c.	chopped white onion
3 to 4	fresh white mushrooms
1 can	straw mushrooms
2	cloves garlic, minced
1 stem	lemongrass (tender portion only), soaked in warm water 20 minutes
3 to 4	Kaffir lime leaves
1 Tbs.	minced fresh Chinese (regular) ginger
1	large, ripe tomato
1 to 2 Tbs.	tomato paste
1 Tbs.	fresh lime juice
1	Galongo Thai ginger, soaked with the lemongrass 20 minutes
1	whole, dried lime (available in Asian markets)
1/2 tsp.	ground coriander
4 c. (1 qt.)	chicken stock
1/2 lb.	raw, shelled shrimp
1/2 lb.	shredded bok choy
	White pepper to taste
3 to 4	green onions, chopped

1. Heat 2 Tbs. canola oil in saucepan. Sauté the onion for 5 minutes.
2. Add the garlic and fresh mushrooms and sauté 5 minutes longer. Add the straw mushrooms.
3. Grate the lemongrass and the Kaffir lime leaves in the food processor and add them to the above mixture, along with the minced Chinese ginger, tomato, tomato paste, and the lime juice. Stir to blend.
4. Add the Galongo ginger in 1/4-inch-thick slices, the whole, dried lime, and the ground coriander. Add the chicken stock and bring to a gentle simmer; cook 20 to 30 minutes. Add the shrimp and simmer 5 minutes longer.

My Way:

Lemongrass: Only the 3-inch white part of the lemongrass stalk should be used. Peel off the tough outer skins.

Ginger: Chinese ginger is available in most produce departments. The best way to keep it is to cut off the knobby parts and wash it well, but don't peel it. Cut it into chunks and process in food processor until grated. Place in a screw-top jar and cover it to the top with dry sherry. This will keep in your refrigerator for several months, ready to be used at a drop of a hat.

5.   Add the bok choy and white pepper. Taste for seasoning. Simmer 3 minutes. Remove the Galongo ginger and the whole, dried lime and discard.

6.   Garnish with chopped green onions and serve.

Evil Jungle Prince with Chicken and Vegetables

The "evil" part of this dish is how spicy you make it. Go easy at first and learn how much or little of the chiles you and your guests like or can handle. Make a double recipe of the sauce and freeze the rest of it for later. Then the sauce will be all ready to go next time. You may substitute shrimp or pork for the chicken.

Serves 4 to 6.

1 lb.	boned and skinned chicken breast
2 to 6	small red chile peppers (depending on hot you like it)
1 stalk	fresh lemongrass
4 to 6	Kaffir lime leaves
4 Tbs.	canola oil
1 c.	coconut milk
1-1/2 Tbs.	tomato paste
1 Tbs.	fish sauce
20 to 30	fresh sweet basil leaves (Thai basil if possible)
1/2 tsp.	salt, optional
1/2 lb.	mixed fresh vegetables (your choice of bell peppers, string beans, water chestnuts, tomatoes, bamboo shoots, miniature corn, asparagus, broccoli, asparagus, zucchini, and mushrooms)
2 c.	chopped cabbage

1. Cut chicken into narrow, 2-inch-long strips.
2. Grind together red peppers, lemongrass, and Kaffir lime leaves in food processor as finely as possible.
3. Heat oil to medium-high and sauté pepper mixture for 3 minutes.
4. Stir in coconut milk and the 1-1/2 Tbs. tomato paste and cook for 2 minutes.
5. Sauté the chicken in a little oil in a sauté pan and then add it to the sauce.
6. Reduce heat to medium-low and stir in fish sauce and the basil. Heat through. Taste for seasoning and add salt if necessary.
7. Sauté the vegetables in 2 Tbs. oil until crisp-tender and add to the chicken and sauce. Serve on a piled-high bed of chopped, raw cabbage with Jasmine Rice to soak up

"We can hold back neither the coming of the flowers

Nor the downward rush of the stream.

Sooner or later, everything comes to its fruition."

— The Tao of Love

all the delicious sauce.

Steamed Jasmine Rice

As the name suggests, this type of rice has a subtle flowery flavor to it. To make a larger batch, double all ingredients except salt, using 1-1/2 tsp. instead.

Serves 4 to 6.

2 c.	water
1 tsp.	salt
1 c.	jasmine rice (purchase at specialty stores)

1. Pour the water into a 1- to 2-quart saucepan and add the salt. Bring to a boil.
2. Add the rice, stir once with a fork, and turn down the heat to simmer. Cover the pan and simmer gently for about 20 minutes or till rice is tender and all of the water has been absorbed.

Pumpkin Crème Brûlée

This French dessert goes very nicely with this Thai meal, I think.

Serves 6.

4 c. (1 qt.)	light cream
2 c.	canned pumpkin purée
6	whole large eggs
1 c.	sugar
1 tsp.	ground cinnamon
1/2 tsp.	ground ginger
1/2 tsp.	ground nutmeg
1/4 c.	packed light brown sugar

1. Preheat oven to 325 degrees. Heat the cream in a saucepan on the stove but do not boil. Combine all other ingredients in a bowl.
2. When the cream comes to a simmer, gradually mix it into the egg and pumpkin mixture and pour into small, oven-proof ramekins. Bake 30 to 40 minutes in a half-inch water bath. Insert knife in the center of custard; if knife comes out clean, the custard is done.
3. Cool the custard completely. Cover with plastic wrap and refrigerate at least 4 hours or overnight.
4. Before serving, place the custards on a cookie sheet and force the brown sugar over the top with a sieve.
5. Place the custards 4 inches from the preheated broiler. Broil till sugar has melted, watching carefully to be sure it does not burn — about 2 minutes.

"Spirit inspires you!"
— D.J.

Asian Menu # 2:

A Blend of Asian Flavors

Scallops with Dipping Sauce
Hanoi Chicken Noodle Soup
Paad Thai Noodles
Kaffir Lime Beef
Spicy Vegetable Stir-Fry
Coconut Pie with Tropical Fruits

Even though these dishes are composed of a blend of several Asian cuisines, the essence of each is carried throughout. The many cultures intertwine, with seafood, chicken, noodles, vegetables, and spices all marrying well to form a whole and compatible menu. The dessert is a Western concoction that nevertheless complements this Asian meal. To me, the blending of foods from different countries and cultures is a view of our food future. I believe we will see and taste more and more blended dishes and menus in the new millennium, as we realize that our spirits and tastes are more closely joined than we ever believed possible. As the globe becomes smaller and smaller, we will freely embrace each other in many ways, beginning with food.

Scallops with Dipping Sauce

An unusual mix of flavors that everyone seems to love. It's a nice addition to an hors d'oeuvres table, too. The walnut butter can be made 2 to 3 days ahead.

Serves 6.

1/2 c.	toasted walnut halves
2 Tbs.	butter, softened
3 Tbs.	fresh lime or lemon juice
1-1/2 Tbs.	soy sauce
2 tsp.	sesame seed
1/4 to 1/2 tsp.	red pepper flakes
6	green onions, thinly sliced
1/3 c.	chopped fresh cilantro or Italian parsley
1-1/2 lbs.	sea scallops

1. Prepare the walnut butter: Place toasted walnuts in food processor together with the softened butter and process until smooth. You should have about 1/4 cup.
2. Make dipping sauce: Blend together the 1/4 c. walnut butter, lime or lemon juice, soy sauce, sesame seed, and red pepper flakes. Set aside.
3. Spread the green onions and cilantro on a serving platter.
4. Pat the scallops dry with paper towels. Coat a large skillet, preferably nonstick, with oil spray and place over moderate heat. Add scallops; stir and toss them in the hot pan for 3 to 4 minutes, until they are lightly browned and cooked through. Do not overcook or they will be tough.
5. Place hot scallops on top of the green onions and cilantro; drizzle with some of the sauce. Pour the remaining sauce into little bowls for individual dipping. Serve with cocktail toothpicks as utensils.

"Stop the water and seize the river.
Take hold of the air and possess the sky.
Such foolish struggle.
To seize the river — become the river.
To possess the sky — become the sky."
— Tao de Ching

Hanoi Chicken Noodle Soup

Serves 6.

8 c.	chicken stock
2 Tbs.	coarsely chopped fresh ginger
3	cloves garlic, peeled
1/2 c.	fresh cilantro leaves
1/2 c.	fresh mint leaves
2	whole chicken breasts, bone in, skin on, as much fat removed as possible
1 lb.	bok choy, chopped
	1/4- to 1/2-inch-wide Vietnamese or Thai rice noodles
3 Tbs.	finely chopped green onions
4 oz.	baby spinach leaves
	Soy sauce to taste
	Vietnamese hot sauce, or other hot sauce

1. In a medium stockpot, bring chicken stock to a simmer over medium heat. Add ginger, garlic, 1/4 c. each cilantro and mint leaves, and chicken. Simmer until chicken is cooked through, about 30 minutes.
2. Remove chicken and allow to cool. Tear each breast into about 6 pieces, discarding the bones and the skin.
3. Strain broth and return to pot over low heat. Add bok choy and simmer 5 minutes.
4. Soak noodles in hot water until softened, 5 to 10 minutes. Cook noodles in boiling water until tender, about 3 minutes. Drain and rinse well under cold water.
5. Divide noodles among six bowls. Add chicken pieces, green onions, remaining mint and cilantro, and the baby spinach. Pour hot broth and bok choy over the top. Season with soy sauce if needed and serve with hot sauce.

Kaffir Lime Beef

Serves 8.

4 Tbs.	canola oil
2	medium white onions, sliced (about 2 cups)
10	Kaffir lime leaves, julienned
10	cloves garlic, sliced thin
2 lbs.	tri-tip beef, cut into strips
	Salt and freshly ground black pepper to taste
8 Tbs.	oyster sauce
4 Tbs.	soy sauce
1 c.	beer
2 c.	water chestnuts, cut in half
2 c.	coarsely chopped fresh basil

1. Preheat oven to 325 degrees. In a large skillet on the stove, heat oil and sauté onions, lime leaves, and garlic.
2. Remove to a heat-proof dish.
3. Add more oil if needed and sauté the beef in batches to seal in the juices and brown lightly. Do not crowd the pan.
4. Add the remaining ingredients except the fresh basil.
5. Bake for 1 hour or till tender.
6. Correct seasoning, stir in the basil, and serve.

"Staying in the present keeps you happy."

— D.J.

Paad Thai Noodles

This dish is so much better when you make it at home. It hasn't been sitting on a steam table for who knows how long, plus I use less oil than restaurants do. It tastes fresher. This makes a big platter, so it's great for a crowd, also good left over with a quick stir-fry a couple nights later.

Serves 10.

3/4 lb.	dried, flat rice noodles (about 1/4- to 1/2-inch wide)
3 Tbs.	fish sauce
3 Tbs.	ketchup
2 Tbs.	rice vinegar
1-1/2 Tbs.	firmly packed brown sugar
1/4 tsp.	cayenne, or to taste (how hot do you like it?)
3	large eggs, lightly beaten
	Canola oil, for sautéing
3/4 lb.	medium shrimp, peeled, deveined, and cut into 1/2-inch pieces
8	garlic cloves, minced
4	large shallots, minced (about 1/2 c.)
3/4 c.	water
3 c.	fresh bean sprouts, rinsed and spun dry
4	green onions, halved lengthwise and cut crosswise into 1-inch pieces
1/4 tsp.	red pepper flakes
1/3 c.	chopped roasted, salted peanuts
	Fresh cilantro sprigs

1. In a large bowl, soak the noodles in warm water to cover for 30 minutes, or until they are softened, and drain them well.
2. In a small bowl stir together the fish sauce, the ketchup, vinegar, brown sugar, and cayenne.
3. Scramble the eggs in a small bowl and cook with a little oil in a small skillet to make an omelet. Turn out onto a cutting board and cool. Roll up and slice into slivers. Set aside.
4. In a wok or large heavy skillet heat 2 to 3 Tbs. oil over moderate heat. Add the shrimp and sauté until pink.
5. Add the garlic and shallots and sauté for 1 to 2 minutes.

"Vulnerability is not a weakness. It is a strength. Very few of us are tough enough to be soft."
— Anonymous

6. Add the fish sauce mixture and stir it into the sautéed ingredients.
7. Add the drained noodles, heating through and stirring.
8. Add the water and continue to cook and stir until piping hot.
9. Add the bean sprouts and green onions, and heat through.
10. Turn the noodles onto a large, heated platter and garnish with the red pepper flakes, peanuts, and cilantro sprigs. Serve immediately to a crowd.

Spicy Vegetable Stir Fry

Serves 4.

1/2 c.	vegetable broth
1/2 c.	fresh broccoli florets
1/2 c.	shredded carrots
2	green onions, sliced fine
2 Tbs.	grated fresh ginger
1/2 tsp.	honey
1/2 to 1 tsp.	red pepper flakes, or to taste
1 Tbs.	hoisin sauce
2 Tbs.	water

1. In a wok or skillet, heat broth to a simmer. Add broccoli and carrots, cooking for 1 minute.
2. Add green onions and cook 2 minutes. Add ginger, honey, and red pepper flakes to taste.
3. Cover and cook 2 minutes or until vegetables are tender-crisp.
4. Stir together hoisin sauce with 2 Tbs. water. Add to vegetables and heat through. Serve over jasmine rice or as a side dish.

The proud cannot be taught. Only the humble can perceive the truth.

Annonymous

Coconut Pie with Tropical Fruits

This dessert is very easy to make, and forms its own crust while baking. Again, it's not really a Thai dessert but blends very well with this or any Asian meal.

Serves 8.

3	large eggs
4 Tbs.	butter, cut into bits
1/2 c.	all-purpose flour
1/2 c.	granulated sugar
2 c.	milk
1/4 tsp.	salt
1/2 tsp.	baking powder
1 tsp.	vanilla extract
3 Tbs.	orange liqueur
1 c.	sweetened, grated coconut

Fresh tropical fruit: Kiwi, pineapple, banana, nectarines, canned lichee nuts and strawberries (even though they are not "tropical" so to speak, they do add nice color.)

1. Preheat oven to 350 degrees. In a blender container, combine all ingredients except fruit. Blend at low speed for 30 seconds, then at high speed for 2 minutes.
2. Pour into a lightly greased 10-inch pie pan and bake for one hour. Test with a knife blade to make sure center is not runny.
3. Cool before serving. Serve a wedge of the pie on individual plates with some of the fruit on the side.

"Take care of today, and tomorrow will take care of itself."

— Anonymous

Asian Menu #3:

A Chinese Feast

Chinese Barbecued Pork
Hot and Sour Soup
Kung Pao Chicken
Pork Fried Rice
Stir-Fried Vegetables
Mandarin Orange Flambé
Sesame Cookies

This is a great meal to prepare with your gourmet club. Everyone can bring the ingredients for one dish and prepare it at the chosen dinner place. That way the guests get to help the host. Remember to bring copies of your recipe to share with everyone. This is a meal for practicing the spirit of togetherness.

Chinese Barbecued Pork

I have made many varieties of BBQ pork, but this is the easiest to fix, and it's delicious. It's so easy that you can feel free to prepare it anytime for an appetizer or for part of an hors d'oeuvre table at the holidays.

Serves 6 as a first course.

1	fresh pork tenderloin
3/4 c.	good-quality hoisin sauce
4 Tbs.	Coleman's dry mustard, mixed to desired consistency with water, or 1/4 c. prepared Chinese hot mustard
1/4 c.	sesame seeds

1. Preheat oven to 325 degrees. Place pork tenderloin on a broiler pan and paint liberally with the hoisin sauce. Bake 45 min. to 1 hour, or till fully cooked. Cool 1 hour.
2. When ready to serve, mix the Coleman's dry mustard with water or white wine to desired thickness (or purchase prepared Chinese hot mustard) and place in a serving bowl or individual, small bowls.
3. Toast the sesame seeds in a dry frying pan till lightly golden. Watch carefully so they do not burn. Place the toasted sesame seeds in individual little serving bowls or one larger bowl.
4. Slice the cooked pork 1/4-inch thick and fan out onto a serving platter. Serve with mustard and sesame seeds on the side.

"WAIT ... Waiting takes courage."

— Scott Peck

Hot and Sour Soup

The preparations of cleaning, chopping, and slicing are a Zen experience for me. You may make this soup a couple of days ahead, refrigerate and then reheat. Do not freeze it, however.

Serves 6.

6	dried Chinese mushrooms, about 1/2-inch in diameter
1/4 c.	canned sliced bamboo shoots
6 oz.	lean pork
6 c.	chicken stock
1-1/2 tsp.	salt
1/2 tsp.	white pepper
1-1/2 tsp.	light soy sauce
3 Tbs.	white vinegar
6	green onions, sliced fine, including the tops
3 Tbs.	cornstarch, mixed with 1/4 c. cold water
1 Tbs.	sesame oil, or to taste (no substitutes)

1. Place dried mushrooms in a small bowl and cover them with warm water. Let soak for 30 minutes, then discard the water.
2. Cut away and discard the tough mushroom stems. To shred the mushroom caps, place them one at a time on a chopping board, cutting thin horizontal slices and then into thin strips.
3. Rinse the bamboo shoots in cold water, drain, and shred them as fine as the mushrooms.
4. Trim all of the fat from the pork and shred it in a similar fashion. Have these ingredients, as well as all the other listed ingredients, prepared ahead of time and set out within easy reach before you begin cooking. This is true of ALL Chinese dishes.
5. Place the chicken stock, salt, soy sauce, mushrooms, bamboo shoots, and pork in a heavy-bottomed saucepan (at least 4-quart capacity) and bring the mixture to a boil over high heat.
6. Reduce the heat to low, cover the pan, and simmer for 3 minutes.

My Way:
There's a lot of "prep" to Chinese cooking – lots of cleaning and slicing. The actual cooking is very easy and quick, but must be done at the last minute. Hint: If you are doing the work yourself, invite no more than 6 people, or it gets to be too much at the end; I learned this the hard way. I once prepared a Chinese dinner for 8 people, and by the time I was finished cooking, serving it, and ready to sit down to join my guests – everyone had already completed the meal! For a larger gathering or less hectic preparation, get everyone to help. Or, just fix a few things with some steamed rice and slim down the "feast" idea. It's up to you and your skill, courage, and energy levels – and spirit, of course.

7. Stir in the white pepper, vinegar, and half of the sliced green onions. Bring the mixture again to a boil. Stir the cornstarch-water mixture until it is smooth and pour it into the boiling soup. Stir constantly until the soup thickens and clears.

8. Taste the soup for seasoning — for a "hotter" flavor, add more white pepper.

9. Pour the soup into a large tureen or individual soup dishes. Stir in some of the sesame oil and sprinkle the remaining green onions over the top. Taste and correct seasoning; serve immediately.

Kung Pao Chicken

This is one of my favorite Chinese dishes. I love the crunch of the peanuts in it and of course the spicy combination of these flavors.

Serves 4 to 6.

1	whole chicken breast, boned, skinned and diced
4 Tbs.	peanut oil
2	cloves garlic, minced
2 tsp.	fresh ginger, minced
1 Tbs.	dry sherry
6 pieces	dried chili pepper
1 tsp.	hot pepper oil (or to taste)
4 Tbs.	green onion, cut on the diagonal
1 Tbs.	peanut butter
1/2 c.	roasted, salted peanuts
1 tsp.	sugar
1 tsp.	soy sauce

1. Sauté the chicken in the heated peanut oil.
2. Mix together all remaining ingredients except for the green onions and peanuts.
3. Add this mixture to the sautéed chicken and heat through, simmer 2 to 3 minutes.
4. Add the onions and peanuts. Heat for 15 seconds and spoon into a serving dish. Serve immediately to 4 to 6 persons, depending on how many dishes you serve.

"A Toast:
To you … who have lived long enough
to hear your own voice
Who will continue to search
Even if you never find
Who will only settle for love."

— D.J.

Pork Fried Rice

This was always my children's favorite Chinese rice dish. Even if we purchased food to go, I always fixed my own fried rice — by popular demand. It became a tradition for us.

Serves 6 to 8.

3-4 c.	cooked long-grain rice, chilled for at least 4 to 6 hours
3	large eggs, for omelet
1/4 c.	peanut or canola oil
1/2 c.	chopped green onions
1 Tbs.	minced fresh Italian parsley
2 to 3 Tbs.	soy sauce
2 slices	cooked ham, diced or julienned
1 c.	thawed frozen peas, drained but not cooked

Chopped green onion tops, for garnish

1. Prepare and chill the rice, or use leftover rice.
2. Make an omelet from the 3 eggs in a little oil, and turn out onto a cutting board. Cool, then roll up and slice the omelet into slivers. Divide and reserve.
3. Heat oil in a large skillet or wok. Add the onions and parsley. Sauté lightly 2 to 3 minutes.
4. Add the cold rice and soy sauce. Stir-fry 10 to 15 minutes to heat through well.
5. Add the ham and the peas; stir and heat through.
6. Add half of the chopped omelet to the rice mixture and stir in well. Taste for seasoning. Turn rice out onto a heated platter or bowl, mounding it. Garnish with remaining omelet and extra chopped green onion tops.

Stir-Fried Vegetables

Once everything is chopped and ready, the rest of the process only takes about 5 minutes. You can use any vegetables or combination thereof that you prefer. Some additional suggestions are baby corn, zucchini, water chestnuts, pea pods, celery, peppers, green onions, mushrooms, etc., etc.,

Serves 6.

Sauce:

4 Tbs.	soy sauce
3 Tbs.	dry sherry
1	clove garlic, minced
1 tsp.	sugar
1 to 2 tsp.	minced fresh ginger
1	small white onion
1/2	green pepper
1/2 lb.	white mushrooms
1	medium-sized tomato
1 c.	broccoli or asparagus
3 to 4 Tbs.	canola oil

1. Mix together all sauce ingredients and set aside.
2. Prepare all vegetables by cleaning and slicing into chunks, on the diagonal.
3. Heat oil to hot in a wok or sauté pan and add the vegetables, one variety at a time, according to which take the longest to cook through.
4. When all vegetables are added and almost cooked to tender-crisp, pour in the sauce and stir to heat through. Serve immediately.

"Spirit guides me always, if I let it."
— D.J.

Mandarin Orange Flambé

Serves 4 to 6.

2 c.	unsweetened coconut
1 qt.	vanilla ice cream, softened slightly and shaped into 3-inch balls

Sauce:

1 can	mandarin oranges, drained
1	fresh orange, peeled and cut into chunks, excluding any white membranes
2/3 c.	fresh-squeezed orange juice
2 Tbs.	brown sugar
	Dash cinnamon
1 to 2 Tbs.	chopped fresh ginger
1/3 c.	brandy

1. Toast the coconut lightly in a dry pan, being careful not to burn it. Cool.
2. Roll the ice cream balls in the cooled, toasted coconut and refreeze in a pretty, clear glass bowl. Cover with plastic wrap and keep in freezer. This is a quick and easy way to serve ice cream; just bring out the whole bowl and place it on the table. The host can serve, or everyone can help themselves by passing the bowl around family style.
3. Make the sauce: Place mandarin oranges and the fresh, cut-up orange in a skillet with the orange juice. Add brown sugar, cinnamon, and ginger and heat through.
4. Add brandy and light immediately with a match or a fire wand.
5. Shake pan over the heat until all of the flames have subsided. Pour over each serving of coconut ice cream balls and serve immediately.

My Way:

If you don't want to do a flamed topping for the ice cream balls, just use a can of lichee nuts in their juice, chilled, as an Asian-style topping.

Sesame Cookies

These cookies are yummy — great with any Asian meal, and can be frozen. The danger is dipping into the freezer for one or two ... or more.

Makes about 3 dozen.

1 c.	butter, softened
2/3 c.	powdered sugar
2 c.	flour
1/4 tsp.	salt
2/3 c.	sesame seeds
1 tsp.	vanilla extract

Topping:

1	large egg yolk
	sesame seeds

1. Preheat oven to 350 degrees. Cream butter and sugar together till smooth; add flour, salt, sesame seed, and vanilla. Mix well. The dough will seem dry at first till well mixed.
2. Shape into balls about the size of a small walnut, flatten with a fork, brush with beaten egg yolk and sprinkle with extra sesame seeds.
3. Bake for 12 to 15 minutes or till lightly golden in color. Cool and serve on the side with the Mandarin Orange Flambé.

*

"Your life is your canvas."
— *Messages from Aurora*

Asian Menu #4:

Dinner Smiling Buddha

Mu Shoo Shrimp
Asian Pork Tenderloin
Jade Noodles
Carrot, Pea Pod and Water Chestnut Stir-Fry
Roasted Bananas with Lime Sauce

This menu is dedicated to one of my favorite spots in Vancouver, British Columbia's Chinatown of the sixties and seventies. The custom at the time was to party and dance until the wee hours of the morning. We would often end the celebration with a large group of us clambering up the long flight of stairs to the Smiling Buddha Restaurant for a late-night or early-morning snack of Chinese food. Through such memories is our spirit enhanced. I treasure them.

Mu Shoo Shrimp

Children love to assemble their own pancakes with these ingredients. Look for the more unusual items at your local Asian market.

Serves 6 to 8.

1 c.	carrots
1 c.	onions
1 c.	fresh mushrooms
1/2 c.	dried Chinese mushrooms, soaked in water and drained
1/3 c.	dried lily buds
1 c.	bean sprouts
1/2 c.	water chestnuts
1/2 Tbs.	minced fresh ginger
1 tsp.	minced garlic
1/2 lb.	shrimp
1 Tbs.	soy sauce
2 tsp.	sesame oil, optional
2	large eggs, beaten
1 pkg.	rice pancakes, thawed (purchase from the freezer section of Asian markets or specialties stores)
	Plum sauce, packaged

1. Cut fresh vegetables julienne style.
2. Precook carrots in a little water.
3. Soak dried mushrooms and lily buds in warm water for 30 minutes. Drain and pat dry. Thinly slice the mushrooms, discarding the stems. Leave the lily buds whole.
4. Heat 2 Tbs. oil in a large pan and cook the onions until limp. Add the carrots, lily buds, bean sprouts, drained water chestnuts, ginger, and garlic. Cook till tender.
5. Add pork and shrimp, soy sauce, and 2 tsp. sesame oil if desired; cook through.
6. Drizzle beaten egg into the above mixture and stir, heating through. Cool, covered; then reheat when ready to serve
7. Heat pancakes, covered, in the microwave. Spread with a spoonful of plum sauce, top with some of the filling and roll up. Serve immediately.

"Have the courage to live life with love."
— Confucius

Asian Pork Tenderloin

Serves 4.

Marinade:
1/4 c.	fresh orange juice
2 Tbs.	oyster sauce
3 Tbs.	light soy sauce
1 Tbs.	sesame oil
1-1/2 tsp.	Chinese five-spice powder
1/2 tsp.	dried thyme
3	cloves garlic, minced

1 lb.	pork tenderloin, trimmed of any fat
	Flour for dredging pork
1 Tbs.	canola oil
2 Tbs.	butter, divided
2	large shallots, chopped fine
1/4 lb.	shiitake mushrooms, stems discarded and caps sliced thin
1/4 c.	brandy
1/4 c.	water
1/3 c.	apricot preserves
1/3 c.	heavy cream

1. Make the marinade: Stir together all marinade ingredients and let stand 15 minutes.
2. Add pork to marinade, tossing to coat completely. Marinate pork, covered and chilled, at least 2 hours or overnight, turning pork at least once.
3. Preheat oven to 200 degrees. Remove pork from marinade and cut into 1-inch-thick slices. In a bowl dredge pork in flour, shaking off excess.
4. In a large heavy skillet, heat the canola oil and 1 Tbs. of the butter over moderately high heat, until hot but not smoking. Sauté pork 5 minutes on each side. Transfer pork to a heat-proof dish and keep warm in middle of oven.
5. To skillet, add remaining 1 Tbs. butter and sauté shallots, stirring, for 1 minute.
6. Add mushrooms and sauté, stirring, 5 minutes, or until the liquid they give off has evaporated.
7. Add brandy and cook mixture, stirring, until liquid is almost evaporated.

8. Add water and preserves, and cook, stirring, until well combined. Stir in cream.
9. Add pork and simmer 5 minutes. Enjoy!

Jade Noodles

Serves 6.

1 lb.	dried spaghetti-style noodles, preferably Chinese
4 qts.	water mixed with 1 Tbs. salt
1	red pepper, stemmed and seeded
1 can	straw mushrooms, drained
1/2 c.	pine nuts
1 Tbs.	cornstarch mixed with 1 Tbs. water, reserved

Sauce:

2	cloves garlic, minced
1 lb.	fresh spinach, stemmed and cleaned
2 bunches	green onion, tops only
16 sprigs	fresh cilantro
12	basil leaves
1/3 c.	chicken stock
2/3 c.	heavy cream
1/2 tsp.	salt
1/4 tsp.	Chinese chili sauce

1. Boil noodles in salted water. Cook till noodles lose their raw taste but are still firm, about 5 minutes. Drain in a colander and rinse under cold water.
2. Cut red pepper into thin slices.
3. Add straw mushrooms and red peppers to the noodles and mix well. Set aside.
4. Toast pine nuts in a dry pan on top of stove. Set aside.
5. Prepare sauce: In a food processor fitted with metal blade, chop garlic, spinach, green onion tops, cilantro, and basil until finely puréed; then add stock, cream, salt, and chili sauce.
6. Purée again; transfer to a bowl and set aside.
7. Place 12-inch skillet over high heat and add sauce to it. Bring sauce to a boil. Add enough of the reserved cornstarch mixture to lightly thicken sauce.
8. Add noodles to sauce and cook until noodles are reheated and red pepper is cooked. Check for seasoning, then serve.

"It takes confidence to change, to move from one time or lifestyle to another, to let some parts of our role, our being fade and other parts to grow and develop."

— D.J.

Carrot, Pea Pod and Water Chestnut Stir-Fry

1/4 c.	peanut oil
1	white onion, sliced on diagonal
1/2 lb.	carrots, peeled and cut into matchsticks
1/2 lb.	pea pods, washed and trimmed
2 cans	sliced water chestnuts

Sauce:

4 Tbs.	soy sauce
3 Tbs.	vermouth
1	clove garlic, crushed
1 tsp.	sugar
2 tsp.	minced fresh ginger

1. Heat oil to medium-high. Add onion and sauté for 1 minute.
2. Add carrots, pea pods, and water chestnuts and stir-fry 3 minutes on medium-high heat.
3. Mix all sauce ingredients together in a small bowl.
4. Add sauce to vegetables and heat till simmering. Serve immediately.

Roasted Bananas with Lime Sauce

Serves 6.

Lime Sauce:

2/3 c.	sugar
1	vanilla bean, split lengthwise
	Grated zest and juice of 6 limes
6 Tbs.	water

Bananas:

8 oz.	unsalted pine nuts, pistachios, walnuts, or pecans
2 c.	cold whole milk
6	whole bananas, just underripe

1. Make lime sauce: Mix together all sauce ingredients in a small saucepan and bring to a boil. Remove from heat and set aside to cool. Remove and discard vanilla bean. Mixture will thicken as it cools.

2. Prepare fruit: Soak the nuts in milk for 1 hour. This hydrates the nuts and enhances their flavor.

3. Preheat oven to 350 degrees. Drain and dry the nuts on a clean towel. Chop nuts roughly and place on a cookie sheet.

4. Peel bananas carefully to avoid breaking them. Gently press each banana into the nuts, coating completely. Place bananas on an ungreased baking sheet and bake 10 to 12 minutes. Remove from oven and cool.

5. To serve, carefully split each banana in fourths lengthwise and fan out on individual serving plates. Ladle the lime sauce on the side.

"There is only one thing in life, and that is the continual renewal of inspiration."

Chapter Seven

Mexico

I have traveled to Mexico at least a dozen times, but I never tire of the cuisine of this marvelous country that is kissed by the sun. As I have mentioned, fire is the universal element that gives us energy and light, and that is the sun's starring role throughout most of Mexico. Besides bringing forth the crops that grace the tables, the sun blesses the spirit of the Mexican people. They have an innocent humility about them, generally speaking, that I find very refreshing. They touch my heart.

Mexican Menu:

A Mexican Fiesta Cinco de Mayo

Mazatlan Prawns with Guacamole
Olive Quesadillas
Fresh Red Salsa
Roasted Green Salsa
Guacamole Salsa
Black Bean Soup
Baked Chiles Rellenos
Flour Tortillas Dulces
Pineapple Soaked in Crème de Menthe

Mexican Independence Day foods are radiant with celebration. This menu may look like a lot of food and prep, but the salsas are not filling, and all of the dishes are easy to make. If you're pressed for time, leave the soup and one of the appetizers for another time.

Mazatlan Prawns with Guacamole

An appetizer that never goes unappreciated by guests.

Serves 8 to 10.

1 lb.	large prawns, raw and in the shell
1 Tbs.	canola oil
1	clove garlic, minced
2 tsp.	fresh lemon juice
	Salt and freshly ground black pepper to taste

1. Peel, devein, and rinse the shrimp in cold water, and drain on paper towels.
2. Heat the oil in a sauté pan.
3. Turn heat to medium-high and add the prawns and the garlic.
4. After 2 to 3 minutes, or when the prawns are pink and just cooked through, add the lemon juice and the salt and pepper. Heat through and serve immediately with Guacamole Salsa, Fresh Red Salsa, and Roasted Green Salsa for dipping.

"Life becomes more and more effortless when I let go of ego."

— D.J.

Fresh Red Salsa

Makes about 2 cups.

1 lb.	fresh, ripe tomatoes
1	medium white onion, chopped
1/2 bunch	fresh cilantro, washed and dried
6	serrano chiles
1 tsp.	salt
1/3 c.	water

1. Finely chop all vegetables. Do not skin the tomatoes and do not seed the chiles.
2. Mix together in a bowl and add the salt and the water, mixing well. Keep refrigerated until ready to serve. Taste for seasoning.

My Way:
Make sure to use rubber gloves when handling hot, spicy chiles!

Roasted Green Salsa

Makes about 4 cups.

12	large tomatillos, husks removed
4	jalapeño chiles
1	yellow onion
1 c.	water
1/2 tsp.	salt
1/2 bunch	fresh cilantro, washed, dried, and chopped
1 tsp.	sugar
1/2	yellow onion, chopped fine

1. Preheat oven to 400 degrees. Wash vegetables. Roast tomatillos and jalapeños along with 1 whole yellow onion for 15 to 20 minutes, till soft.
2. Blend the vegetables in the food processor with water, salt, cilantro, and sugar.
3. Pour into container and add the chopped, raw onion. Mix and serve.
4. May store in refrigerator for 2 weeks. Use as a garnish with grilled or baked meats as well as a dip for chips.

Guacamole Salsa

Serves 8 to 10.

3	large, ripe black-skinned avocados
3	cloves garlic, minced
2 Tbs.	sweet, white onion, minced
2 tsp.	fresh lime juice
1 Tbs.	extra-virgin olive oil
1 tsp.	salt
1/2 tsp.	dried, crushed red pepper, or to taste
1/2 tsp.	ground cumin
1 tsp.	chopped fresh cilantro

1. Peel and cube the avocados in a bowl, reserving one of the seeds.
2. Add the remaining ingredients and mash by hand. Leave the salsa lumpy.
3. Put the reserved avocado seed in a bowl and pour the guacamole over it. The seed prevents the salsa from turning dark. Discard it just before serving.
4. Serve as a condiment with seafood, meats, and chicken, taco chips, or as a spread for sandwiches.

"If fear sets in, get busy."
— Anonymous

Olive Quesadillas

Serves 6.

6	flour or corn tortillas
1 c.	shredded mozzarella cheese (about 4 oz.)
2/3 c.	feta cheese, crumbled
1/4 c.	chopped, toasted walnuts
1/4 c.	chopped, pitted ripe olives
2 tsp.	chopped fresh oregano, or 1/2 tsp. dried
1 Tbs.	extra-virgin olive oil
	Salsa

1. To soften tortillas, wrap in plastic wrap and microwave for a short time — 30 to 60 seconds.
2. Combine cheeses, nuts, olives, and oregano: Spread onto half of each tortilla.
3. Fold quesadillas in half and secure with toothpicks. Brush one side with oil or use oil spray.
4. In a skillet cook quesadillas, oil side down, over medium-low heat for about 4 minutes, brushing with oil and turning once. Serve with salsa.

Black Bean Soup

Makes 4 quarts; freezes well.

1/4 lb.	bacon, coarsely chopped
1/2 lb.	black beans, rinsed and soaked overnight in water
2 qts.	cold water
1/2	yellow onion, chopped fine
1/4 c.	celery
1/4 c.	chopped carrot
2	garlic cloves, minced
1/2 tsp.	ground white pepper
1 tsp.	salt
1 tsp.	ground cumin
1	bay leaf
1 tsp.	dried oregano

1. Sauté bacon bits and reserve.
2. Place all other ingredients into a large pot and bring to a boil. Reduce heat and simmer until cooked, about 2-1/2 hours.
3. Remove beans from heat and purée in food processor till smooth. Thin with chicken stock if necessary.
4. Add the bacon bits and serve or freeze.

Baked Chiles Rellenos

An easy way to make rellenos as opposed to the classic fried version. The taste is all there with a smooth, soufflé-like texture.

Serves 8.

16	large, fresh poblano chiles
1/2 lb.	sharp cheddar cheese, grated
1/2 lb.	Monterey jack cheese, grated
1 can	evaporated milk (5-1/2 oz. can)
3	large egg yolks, lightly beaten
3 Tbs.	flour
	Salt and freshly ground black pepper
4	large egg whites
	Pinch cream of tartar

Chopped fresh cilantro

1. Preheat oven to 325 degrees. Wash, core, and seed the fresh chiles, and set aside on paper towels. Place on a dish and steam, covered, in microwave oven.
2. Mix half of the cheddar and half the jack cheese together in a bowl. Stuff the peppers with the cheese mixture and place in the bottom of an large, oiled baking dish.
3. Sprinkle the remaining cheeses on top of the chiles.
4. In a bowl combine the evaporated milk and egg yolks, and whisk in the flour; salt and pepper to taste.
5. In another bowl, beat the egg whites with the cream of tartar and a pinch of salt until they hold stiff peaks but are not dry.
6. Fold into the milk and yolk mixture. Spoon this mixture over the chiles.
7. Bake the rellenos for 45 minutes or until puffy and brown. Serve with hot corn tortillas and salsa.

"Study and practice humility. This is very difficult to do sometimes."

— D.J.

Flour Tortillas Dulces

These are very popular and get gobbled up fast. If there are any left, keep them in an air-tight container at room temperature for a few days for future use.

Serves 10 or more.

6 to 8   flour tortillas
Canola oil for deep frying
Sugar and cinnamon, for dusting

1. Heat oil to approximately 360 degrees. Cut flour tortillas into small pieces and deep fry in the hot oil till golden. Be careful not to burn yourself or spill any oil on the stove.
2. Remove with a slotted spoon to a cookie sheet lined with paper towels. Drain well.
3. While the tortillas are still hot, sprinkle liberally with the sugar and cinnamon. Serve with the pineapple marinated in the crème de menthe.

"Spirit fills my heart with inner peace."

Pineapple Soaked in Crème de Menthe

Simple and delicious!

Serves 8 to 10.

1	medium-sized ripe pineapple, peeled, cored, and cut into cubes
1/2 c.	crème de menthe

1. Combine the two ingredients in a bowl and chill until ready to serve.

Chapter Eight

The American Pacific Northwest

This section is comprised of dishes and recipes adapted from cuisines around the world as well as from my home, the U.S. Pacific Northwest. Classic ethnic flavors pair well with the fruits of the land and neighboring sea of Oregon, Washington, and northern California — such as clams, salmon, crab, and a variety of rockfish, fresh vegetables, and berries. A selection from the assortment of good Northwestern wines available enhances any meal made with these local ingredients..

What excites me about the Northwest is the liberal attitude that prevails here — not just in politics and lifestyle, but toward food as well. It shows in the local home cook who says, "Hey, why not blend foods from different countries in one meal?" And it is expressed by the chef who says, "Let's add some Asian touches, like ginger, to our regional salads or fish." This sentiment has built over the decades, and today Northwesterners enjoy a palate as limitless as the imagination, and actually gravitate toward creating and trying the unusual and the new. This area is truly, for me, the home of Cooking with Spirit.

Pacific Northwest Menu #1:

A Summer Dinner in Astoria

Olive Crostini
Shrimp Gaspacho
Crab Cakes with Roasted Red Pepper Sauce
Duchesse Potatoes
Oregon Floating Islands in Custard

Astoria, Oregon, is a charming coastal town with spectacular ocean vistas, situated at the confluence of the mighty Columbia River and the Pacific Ocean. Astoria's rich seaport history lives on, as evidenced by some of the classic Victorian homes and the abundance of fresh seafood here. I love driving over the long, long bridge connecting Astoria to the Long Beach Peninsula of Washington — I feel like I'm flying just above the water. Taste some the adventurous spirit of this area as you sample my Crab Cakes with Roasted Red Pepper Sauce and Oregon Floating Islands in Custard.

Olive Crostini

Serves 8 to 10.

1/2 c.	pitted black olives
1/2 c.	green, pimento-stuffed olives
2	cloves garlic, peeled
1/2 c.	grated Parmesan cheese
2 Tbs.	butter
1 Tbs.	extra-virgin olive oil
1/2 c.	grated Monterey jack cheese
1/4 c.	minced fresh Italian parsley
1	long loaf baguette bread

1. In food processor fitted with steel blade, coarsely chop both types of olives. Transfer to a bowl.
2. With the motor running, drop peeled garlic cloves through the feed tube and process till finely minced.
3. Add Parmesan cheese, butter, and olive oil; process into a paste, adding a little more oil if necessary. Mixture should not be dry but should be thick enough to spread. Add to olive mixture and mix well. Fold in jack cheese and parsley.
4. Cut baguette into thin slices. Spread each slice liberally with the olive spread.
5. Broil until bubbly and lightly browned. Serve immediately.

My Way:
You may also toast the bread slices alone, sprayed with olive oil, in a 350-degree oven until crisp and golden; then serve the spread on the side. Great for picnics – and the leftover olive spread is terrific on pizza or in omelets.

Shrimp Gazpacho

This recipe was given to me by Virginia Plainfield many years ago. Of course, each of us have changed it to our own liking. This is simply the best chilled soup ever, and it couldn't be easier to prepare. Take it on a picnic and serve in mugs or plastic cups.

Serves 4.

1 qt.	Clamato juice
1/2 c.	peeled and diced cucumber, large seeds removed
1/3 c.	chopped green onion, white and green parts
4 oz.	cooked bay shrimp, or larger fresh shrimp cut in half
2 Tbs.	canola oil
2 Tbs.	red wine vinegar
2 tsp.	sugar
1 Tbs.	minced fresh dill, or 1 tsp. dried
1	clove garlic, minced
4 oz.	regular (not low-fat) cream cheese, cubed
1	ripe avocado, peeled and diced
1/4 tsp.	Tabasco sauce, or to taste

1.   Mix all ingredients well in a bowl and chill 45 minutes or more before serving.

Crab Cakes with Roasted Red Pepper Sauce

These are delicious as either a main course or as appetizers. For appetizers, make 2-inch instead of 4-inch cakes. These are similar to the crab cakes served at the historic Heathman Hotel in Portland, Oregon.

Serves 6.

Red Pepper Sauce:

3	medium red bell peppers, diced into 1-inch pieces
3	cloves garlic, minced
4 Tbs.	dry white wine
	Dash freshly ground black pepper

Crab Cakes:

24 oz. lump	Dungeness crab meat, picked over for shells
2 c.	soft bread crumbs
1 c.	diced red bell pepper
2	large eggs, beaten
2	Tbs. mayonnaise
2 tsp.	Dijon mustard
1/4 tsp.	dry mustard
	Dash white pepper
6 drops	Tabasco sauce
2 Tbs.	chopped fresh Italian parsley
1-1/2 c.	toasted bread crumbs

1. Make the red pepper sauce: Preheat oven to 400 degrees. Spray a shallow, 1-quart casserole with nonstick cooking spray.
2. Add pepper pieces, garlic, and white wine. Cover casserole and bake 20 minutes or until peppers are soft, stirring once.
3. In the bowl of food processor fitted with steel blade, process bell pepper mixture till smooth.
4. Season with black pepper. Makes 1-1/2 cups.
5. Make the crab cakes: In a large bowl combine crab, bread crumbs, diced bell peppers, and eggs. Stir well. Add mayonnaise, Dijon mustard, dry mustard, white pepper, Tabasco sauce, and parsley. Stir gently.

If a little dreaming is dangerous, the cure for it is not to dream less but to dream more, to dream all the time.

Marcel Proust

6.   Shape into twelve 4-inch, round patties. Carefully cover the patties with the toasted bread crumbs and place on a plate. Cover with plastic wrap and chill 30 to 60 minutes. They will hold their shape better this way.

7.   Sauté in a lightly oiled nonstick pan till golden brown and cooked through. To serve, pool some red pepper sauce on each individual plate. Place 2 crab cakes over the pepper sauce and serve immediately with Duchesse Potatoes.

Duchesse Potatoes

This recipe takes the lowly potato to high cuisine, definitely worthy of the company of crab cakes. You'll find the recipe for Duchesse Potatoes in the French portion of this book (see page 103).

Oregon Floating Islands in Custard Sauce

Serve this impressive, two-part dessert Oregon style, with whole, fresh, seasonal berries.

Serves 6.

Berries:

1-3/4 lbs.	mixed berries, such as raspberries, strawberries, blackberries, boysenberries, or blueberries, or any combination thereof
1/2 c.+ 2 Tbs.	sugar
3/4 c.	water
1/4 c. + 2 tsp.	potato starch
3-1/2 Tbs.	cognac
3-1/2 Tbs.	Kirsch
3-1/2 Tbs.	Madeira

1. Wash and trim berries. Place them in a saucepan with the sugar and 3/4 c. water and bring to a boil. Simmer for 15 minutes.
2. Purée the berries in a food processor.
3. In a small bowl, mix together the cognac, Kirsch, and Madeira.
4. Dissolve the potato starch in the liquors and add berry purée.
5. Return mixture to the saucepan and bring to a boil again. Simmer 10 minutes.
6. Pour mixture into 6 individual molds or little glass bowls and cover with plastic wrap. Refrigerate overnight.

Remainder:

1 recipe	Vanilla Custard (found in the Italian section of this book)
	Whole, fresh berries, for garnish

1. Prepare and chill the custard.
2. To serve, remove berry molds from refrigerator, and dip the bottoms of the molds into hot water for 5 seconds. Unmold fruit onto 6 individual dessert plates. Surround with custard and fresh berries scattered over all.

*

Pacific Northwest Menu #2:

A Barbecue at Gleneden Beach

Shrimp Pâté
Tossed Greens with Tomatoes and Artichoke Hearts
Broiled Flank Steak with Marinara Sauce
Vermicelli and Pesto
Iced Lemon Zest Souffle

The central Oregon Coast means rugged cliffs, salt marshes, and sandy beaches that stretch forever. Over the years, I have spent many, many summer and winter retreats at beautiful Gleneden Beach. Watching a perfect sunset, listening to the sounds of the ocean, and barbecuing this fragrant flank steak at the end of the day is hard to beat. I think to myself, "Ah, isn't life wonderful!" Baked potatoes go equally as well as pasta with the flank steak, which is everybody's favorite. The iced lemon soufflé — a total departure from the rest of the menu — is light and elegant. You can freeze it several weeks ahead of time and bring it out at the end of a delicious and satisfying meal.

Shrimp Pâté

Serves 8 to 10 as appetizers.

8 oz.	low-fat cream cheese
6 oz.	cooked small bay shrimp (buy them precooked at the seafood counter of your grocery store)
1 Tbs.	chopped green onions
1-1/4 c.	grated sharp cheddar cheese
2 tsp.	Worcestershire sauce
3 drops	Tabasco sauce
1 tsp.	fresh lemon juice
2 Tbs.	mayonnaise

1. Combine all the ingredients well, place into a serving crock or bowl and chill.
2. Serve with fresh vegetables and crackers.

"We must not kill our enemies, but kill their desire to kill."

— Ghandi

Tossed Greens with Tomatoes and Artichoke Hearts

Serves 6.

1 head	romaine lettuce, washed, dried and torn into bite-size pieces
2	medium, ripe tomatoes, washed and cut into wedges
1 jar	marinated artichoke hearts (about 1 cup)
1/2 c.	slivered red onion

Dressing:

2 Tbs.	red wine vinegar
1 tsp.	Dijon mustard
1	garlic clove, minced
1/2 tsp.	salt
	Freshly ground black pepper
1 Tbs.	fresh mixed herbs, such as Italian parsley, basil, and thyme
6 Tbs.	extra-virgin olive oil
1 c.	garlic croutons, homemade or packaged

1. Place all the vegetables into a large salad bowl.
2. Mix all the dressing ingredients except for the oil in a small bowl with a wire whisk to blend.
3. Slowly add the olive oil and whisk to blend. Toss with the salad and serve immediately with garlic croutons on top.

Broiled Flank Steak with Marinara Sauce

This recipe for grilled steak is another that appeals to every palate. If any is left over, it's great in a steak sandwich the next day with some good mustard. It's very easy to prepare and fool proof. Also I like flank steak for its good flavor and low fat content. You'll find the Marinara Sauce recipe in the Italian section of this book, under "Linguine with Scallops Marinara."

Serves 4 to 6.

1 Tbs.	canola oil
1 Tbs.	extra-virgin olive oil
2 Tbs.	minced fresh Italian parsley
1/2 tsp.	salt
1 tsp.	freshly ground black pepper
1	large clove garlic, minced
1/2 lb.	white mushrooms, cleaned and sliced
1	flank steak (about 2 to 3 lbs.)

1. Preheat the broiler. Mix all ingredients except steak together in a bowl.
2. Spread half the mixture onto one side of the flank steak.
3. Place steak, oil side up, on greased broiler pan. Broil 4 to 5 minutes or till blood rises to the top.
4. Turn steak over and spread the rest of oil mixture over the steak. Broil 3 to 4 minutes longer or till done medium-rare. Cut into thin, diagonal slices, with the grain.
5. Sauté mushrooms quickly on high, just until golden brown and heated through — do not overcook. If they expel their juices, turn the heat up some so they'll brown nicely.
6. Place some of the meat on each plate, top with the marinara sauce and some sautéed mushrooms, and serve the Vermicelli and Pesto on the side.

"There are no mistakes, only unexpected results."
— Anonymous

Vermicelli and Pesto

I like very thin, round noodles — not the thick, starchy kind. Thinner varieties of pasta are more delicate-tasting, letting the flavor of the sauce come through. In this case, the addition of Parmesan cheese adds to the complexity of the pesto.

Serves 4 to 6.

Pesto:

2 c.	fresh basil, leaves only
3/4 c.	extra-virgin olive oil
1	large clove garlic
1 tsp.	salt
1/2 tsp.	freshly ground black pepper
2 Tbs.	pine nuts
1/3 c.	Parmesan cheese
1 lb.	dried vermicelli, capellini, or very thin (#20) spaghetti noodles
	Large pot boiling water mixed with 2 tsp. salt
1 to 2 Tbs.	extra-virgin olive oil

1. Place basil, garlic, salt and pepper, and 1/4 c. olive oil into the bowl of the food processor. Blend to smooth.
2. Blend, and slowly add the remaining 1/2 c. olive oil.
3. Add the pine nuts and mix with on-and-off motion till nuts are slightly chopped but not pulverized. I like them chunky.
4. Place the mixture into a bowl and stir in the cheese.
5. Cook the pasta in the pot of boiling, salted water until al dente.
6. Drain, rinse in hot water, and drain well again. Toss the pasta with the 2 Tbs. olive oil.
7. Toss with the pesto sauce and serve immediately.

My Way:

In basil season I make several batches of this pesto sauce and put it in plastic containers in my freezer, so that I can have fresh pesto sauce all winter. It's great with grilled meats of all kinds as well as seafood, especially grilled, large scampi shrimp ... also on crostini for an appetizer, inside omelets, in scrambled eggs, and as a spread for sandwiches. The list goes on and on.

Iced Lemon Zest Soufflé

This dessert is nice and light after such a satisfying meal. It can be made ahead, frozen for up to 3 weeks, and then brought out just before serving. Just remember to wrap it well so that it stays fresh. Place in refrigerator 1 hour before serving.

Pastry Cream Custard:

3/4 c.	milk
2	large egg yolks
1/3 c.	sugar
2 Tbs.	cornstarch

Soufflé:

3/4 c.	fresh lemon juice
	Finely grated zest of 4 lemons
1 c.	egg whites, room temperature
1 c.	sugar
3 c.	heavy cream
	Lemon slices, for garnish

"The only way out is through."

— Robert Frost

1. Make pastry cream custard: In heavy saucepan, heat milk to scalding.
2. Beat egg yolks in a bowl until light. Add sugar and cornstarch slowly.
3. Pour in hot milk and beat until light and foamy.
4. Return to saucepan or double boiler. Cook, stirring constantly with a wire whisk, until mixture is thick and smooth. Pour the sauce into a bowl, and set this in a larger bowl filled with ice to cool.
5. Make the soufflé: Mix lemon juice and zest into the custard.
6. In separate bowl, beat egg whites, adding sugar slowly. Beat until very stiff.
7. In separate bowl, beat heavy cream until stiff.
8. Fold the pastry cream into the egg whites, then fold in whipped cream. Pour into a lightly oiled, 2-quart soufflé dish. Chill 12 hours or set in freezer 2 to 3 hours.
9. Decorate the top with thinly sliced lemon twists. Or, in a clear glass soufflé dish, place thin, flat slices of lemon around the inside edge of the bowl before adding soufflé mixture. Serve or freeze for later.

Pacific Northwest Menu #3:

A Velvet and Diamonds City Dinner for Four

Coconut Shrimp
Fennel Soup with Garlic Croutons
Beef Filet with Merlot Sauce
Oven-Roasted Vegetables
Tossed Mixed Greens in Lime Dressing
Florida Key Lime Pie

This dinner is about elegance and romance. Dress up. Be Sensuous. Light the candles. Put on some mood music, your choice of jazz, or maybe some rhythm and blues. Dim the lights, float the flowers, and soak in the variety of flavors in this menu. Good for the soul, and good for the spirit!

Coconut Shrimp

An appetizer fit for a star-studded evening.

Serves 10.

Spice Mix:

1 to 2 Tbs.	cayenne pepper
1-1/4 tsp.	salt
1-1/2 tsp.	Hungarian paprika
1-1/2 tsp.	freshly ground black pepper
1-1/4 tsp.	garlic powder
3/4 tsp.	onion powder
3/4 tsp.	oregano
3/4 tsp.	thyme

Dipping Sauce:

1 scant c.	orange marmalade
2-1/2 Tbs.	Dijon mustard
2-1/2 Tbs.	creamy horseradish

Shrimp:

2 lbs.	large shrimp (40 shrimp)
1 Tbs.	canola oil
1 Tbs.	butter
2 c.	flaked, sweetened coconut, toasted

1. Place spice mix ingredients in a screw-top jar and shake up. Store extra in refrigerator.
2. Mix together dipping sauce ingredients and set aside.
3. Peel and devein the shrimp, and coat with 2 Tbs. of the spice mix.
4. Sauté the shrimp in 1 Tbs. oil and 1 Tbs. butter until pink and firm to the touch.
5. Remove from pan and serve warm or chilled, with the dipping sauce on the side in one bowl and the toasted coconut in another. To eat: Using a toothpick as a skewer, dip each shrimp first into the dipping sauce and then roll in the coconut.

My Way:

Toast coconut in a dry sauté pan 5 to 8 minutes, till golden. Watch carefully so coconut does not burn, stirring often.

Fennel Soup with Garlic Croutons

Serves 4 to 6.

Garlic Croutons :

1	head garlic
1 tsp.	extra-virgin olive oil
4 to 6 slices	Italian bread, 1/2-inch thick

Soup:

3	large fennel bulbs (about 2 to 3 lbs. total)
3 Tbs.	extra-virgin olive oil
2 Tbs.	butter
3	medium leeks, cleaned and coarsely chopped (white part only)
6 to 7 c.	chicken stock
	Salt and freshly ground black pepper to taste
1/3 c.	grated Parmesan cheese

1. Prepare the garlic croutons: Preheat the oven to 400 degrees. Remove most of the papery outer skin of the garlic, but leave the head intact.

2. Cut 1/2 inch off the top of the garlic head and discard; drizzle rest of garlic head with 1 tsp. olive oil and wrap in aluminum foil. Place in the oven and bake for 45 minutes or until garlic is very soft.

3. Meanwhile place the bread on a baking sheet in the oven and toast until lightly golden. Remove bread from oven and set aside.

4. When the garlic head is cool enough to handle, squeeze the individual cloves out of the bulb into a small bowl. Mash the garlic with a fork and set aside.

5. Make the soup: Slice fennel bulbs crosswise into thin slices. Heat the oil and butter in a large saucepan over medium-high heat.

6. Add the fennel and leeks and sauté until softened, 5 to 7 minutes.

7. Add the stock and bring to a boil. Reduce the heat and simmer, loosely covered, until the vegetables are very soft, 20 to 25 minutes.

8. Remove 1 c. of the vegetables, and purée them in a blender. Stir the purée back into the soup and simmer just until heated through, 1 or 2 minutes. Season with salt and pepper.

"Because I love, there is an invisible way across the sky. Birds travel by that way. The sun and the moon and all the stars travel that path by night."

— Raine

9. Spread the toasted bread crouton slices with the garlic purée.

10. To serve, place a piece of the toast in the bottom of each soup bowl. Ladle soup over the toast and sprinkle Parmesan cheese over the top; serve immediately.

Beef Fillet with Merlot Sauce

Serves 4.

1 c.	beef broth
1/2 c.	merlot or other dry red wine
2 Tbs.	seedless raspberry jam
1/2 tsp.	freshly ground black pepper
4	thin slices pancetta ham (about 4 oz. total)
4	beef tenderloin steaks (about 1-1/2 inches thick)
	Salt
	Freshly ground black pepper

1. Preheat broiler or prepare barbecue coals. In a 1- to 2-quart pan over high heat, stir together broth, merlot, jam, and pepper until boiling, then boil until reduced to 2/3 c. This takes approximately 7 minutes. Do not cover the pan.

2. Unroll pancetta and wrap a slice around the rim of each tenderloin.

3. Broil steaks on a rack in a pan 4 to 6 inches from heat until browned, 6 to 7 minutes; or barbecue 4 to 6 inches above hot coals.

4. Turn steaks over and broil until tops are browned, 6 to 7 minutes more for rare, longer if medium or well done.

5. Put steaks on warm plates and spoon sauce over them. Add salt to taste if necessary. Pass the pepper mill.

Oven Roasted Vegetables

Roasted vegetables are simple to prepare and work well with almost any meal. We have such an abundance of fresh produce that we never have an excuse not to eat lots of good, fresh vegetables. These make great leftovers by just zapping quickly in the microwave. You may use any variety: zucchini, parsnips, green beans, asparagus, cauliflower, sweet potatoes, etc.

Serves 6 to 8.

3 Tbs.	extra-virgin olive oil
1	large white onion, peeled and cut into chunks (all of the vegetables in each batch should be about the same size)
3	carrots, peeled and cut into chunks
6 to 8	red potatoes, scrubbed and cut into halves, or quarters if they are larger 2 yams, peeled and cut into chunks
20	garlic cloves, unpeeled
2 Tbs.	fresh, minced rosemary, or 2 tsp. dried
2 Tbs.	fresh, minced thyme, or 2 tsp. dried
1-1/4 tsp.	salt
	Freshly ground black pepper to taste
1 small bunch	broccoli, cut into chunks
8	mushrooms, halved, quartered, or left whole, depending on their size
2	red peppers, cut into chunks
1	green or yellow pepper, cut into chunks

1. Preheat oven to 425 degrees.
2. Place first 6 ingredients into a large bowl. Toss all to coat with the olive oil.
3. Add the herbs, salt and pepper, and toss again.
4. Spray a large jelly-roll pan with nonstick cooking spray and place the vegetable mixture on it. Drizzle with another Tbs. or so of olive oil.
5. Roast for about 20 to 25 minutes on middle rack of oven, stirring once or twice.
6. Add remaining vegetables to the pan and stir. Bake 20 to 30 minutes longer and test for doneness. When vegetables are uniformly tender, serve immediately.

"You need attend only to where you are going, not to where you have been."
— Anonymous

Tossed Mixed Greens in Lime Dressing

With this meal, I like to serve the salad last. You could also serve a cheese board on the side, in the French manner.

Serves 4 to 6.

| 1 head | red leaf lettuce, washed and dried |
| 1 head | butter lettuce, washed and dried |

Dressing:

1/2 c.	extra-virgin olive oil
3 Tbs.	fresh lime juice
1 tsp.	grated lime zest (green part only)
1/2 tsp.	salt
	Freshly ground black pepper

| 1/4 c. | walnut halves, toasted |

1. Place greens in a salad bowl and chill until serving time.
2. Place dressing ingredients in a screw-top jar and shake well. Chill until serving time.
3. When ready, toss the greens with some of the dressing, top with some toasted walnut halves, and serve immediately.

Florida Key Lime Pie

The secret to an authentic-tasting lime pie is using fresh Key limes or Key lime juice.

Serves 8.

1-1/2 c.	graham cracker crumbs
7 Tbs.	melted butter
7	large egg yolks
1 can	sweetened, condensed milk (14-oz. can)
3/4 tsp.	cream of tartar
1/2 tsp.	finely grated lime zest, preferably from the petite yellow key limes from the Florida Keys, or the more common green Persian limes.
3/4 c.	Nellie and Joe's Key West brand lime juice, or fresh lime juice
1 c.	heavy cream, whipped stiff with 1 tsp. vanilla extract and 3 Tbs. powdered sugar

"Those who are willing to be vulnerable move among mysteries."
— Rothke

1. Preheat oven to 350 degrees. Make the crust: In a small bowl, stir together the graham cracker crumbs and melted butter until well blended. Spray a 9-inch pie pan with nonstick cooking spray, and press the crumb mixture firmly over the bottom and sides of pie pan. Bake the pie shell for 5 to 7 minutes.
2. In a medium mixing bowl, whip the egg yolks until foamy, about 3 minutes.
3. Add cream of tartar and condensed milk, and blend for about 1 minute.
4. Pour the lime juice and zest into the egg mixture, and mix for about 1 minute.
5. Pour filling into the prepared crust. The liquid should reach the top of the pie pan. Bake in the preheated oven for 20 minutes. Cool for 15 minutes, and then refrigerate until ready to serve.
6. Just before you are ready to serve, garnish with the sweetened whipped cream by piping it over the top or sides of the pie in a decorative pattern.

Pacific Northwest Menu #4:

A Dinner on the Willamette River

Crab Cakes on Cornmeal Biscuits
Mixed Greens with Toasted Filberts and Pears
Salmon Escalopes with Cilantro
Nutted Wild Rice
Julienne of Fresh, Braised vegetables
Pear and Pine Nut Cake

I lived on the shore of the Willamette River for years and served this dinner to friends and students many times. The water was so soothing, with lots of green trees and blue sky all around. All of the earth elements were present there, and everyone felt nurtured and blessed, encompassed by all that natural spirit. I believe that whenever you need to get more in touch with spirit, you should involve yourself with nature. We in the Pacific Northwest have a great respect and appreciation for the natural beauty surrounding us, and it shows in our cooking — and especially in this particular menu.

Crab Cakes on Cornmeal Biscuits

I included this recipe for crab because it is wonderful as an hors d'oeuvre that you can pick up with your hands — refined finger food!

Makes 3 dozen each appetizer-size crab cakes and biscuits.

Tartar Sauce:

2 c.	mayonnaise (preferably homemade)
2 Tbs.	white wine vinegar
3	sweet gherkins, minced
3	green onions, minced
1/4 c. + 2 Tbs.	capers, drained and rinsed

Cornmeal Biscuits:

4	medium jalapeño peppers, seeded and quartered
1-3/4 c. + 2 Tbs.	flour
1-1/4 c.	yellow cornmeal
4 tsp.	baking powder
1 Tbs.	sugar
1-1/2 tsp.	salt
1	large egg
1 c.	milk
3 Tbs.	canola oil

Crab Cakes:

1/2 lb. lump	Dungeness crabmeat, picked over for shells, rinsed and drained
1-1/2 c.	fresh, soft bread crumbs
1	green onion, finely chopped
1 Tbs.	chopped fresh Italian parsley
1	large egg, lightly beaten
1/4 c.	mayonnaise
2 tsp.	Dijon mustard
2 tsp.	fresh lemon juice
1/4 tsp.	Worcestershire sauce
1/4 tsp.	salt
	Freshly ground black pepper to taste
	Canola oil

My Way:

When I bake these biscuits, I freeze the extras for a week or two and serve with other fillings such as ham and mustard; pesto and ham; cheese, heated to melting, along with some good chutney; or avocado and bacon. Come up with your own favorite combinations with these delicious biscuits.

1. Make the tartar sauce: In a small bowl combine all tartar sauce ingredients. Cover and refrigerate until cold. Keeps 1 week.

2. Prepare the biscuits: Preheat oven to 350 degrees. Place jalapeño peppers and dry ingredients in a food processor and pulse to combine. Add remaining biscuit ingredients and process until combined.

3. Remove dough from bowl and place on a floured surface. Knead 2 or 3 times. Pat or roll dough into a 1/2-inch-thick circle. Using a 1-1/2 — inch cutter, cut out as many biscuits as possible, flouring cutter frequently to prevent sticking. Gather up scraps into a ball, flatten, and cut until finished.

4. Line a baking sheet with parchment paper and place biscuits 1 inch apart. Bake in lower third of oven for 15 minutes.

5. Remove biscuits from oven and transfer to a wire rack to cool.

6. Prepare the crab cakes: In a medium bowl combine all crab cake ingredients except the oil.

7. Using 2 tsp. of the mixture for each cake, form into 1/4-inch-thick patties. Crab cakes may be refrigerated at this point for up to 6 hours.

8. In a large heavy skillet over medium-high heat, heat a small amount of oil until hot and cook the crab cakes until brown on bottom, about 1 minute. Turn and cook until brown on other side, about 45 seconds. Drain on paper towels.

9. To serve, split biscuits in half horizontally. Place a crab cake on bottom half of each biscuit. Top with a generous amount of tartar sauce and replace top half of biscuit.

Mixed Greens with Toasted Filberts and Pears

"Filbert" is the local moniker for hazelnut.

Serves 6.

Dressing:

1/4 c.	fresh lemon juice
1 Tbs.	white wine vinegar
1/2 tsp.	Dijon mustard
2	garlic cloves, minced
1/4 c.	extra-virgin olive oil
2 Tbs.	grape seed oil
1/4 tsp.	freshly ground black pepper

Salad:

1/2 head	Romaine lettuce, cleaned, dried, and torn into bite-size pieces
1/2 head	red leaf lettuce, cleaned, dried, and torn into bite-size pieces
1	red Bartlett pear, sliced thin
1/3	red onion, sliced into thin half-rings
1/2	yellow pepper, seeded and sliced thin
1/2 c.	croutons
1/2 c.	grated Romano cheese
1/2 c.	coarsely chopped toasted filberts (hazelnuts)

1. Combine all of the dressing ingredients in a screw - top jar and shake well.
2. Place the lettuce in a large salad bowl. Add the pear, red onion, and yellow pepper to the lettuce. Toss gently. Add the croutons and the grated Romano cheese and toss well, with some of the dressing.
3. Place on individual salad plates and top with the toasted filberts.

Salmon Escalopes with Cilantro

"Escalopes" are thin slices of boneless salmon, cut across the grain. They are similar in thickness to veal scallops, about 1/4- to 1/2-inch thick.

Serves 8.

1/2 c.	flour for dipping the salmon
	Salt and freshly ground black pepper to taste
16	salmon escalopes, 1-1/2 oz. each, or 8 small fillets, about 3 oz. each
4 Tbs.	butter
4 Tbs.	light soy sauce
2 Tbs.	fresh lemon juice
6 Tbs.	chopped fresh cilantro or Italian parsley

1. Place the flour and salt and pepper on a plate and mix thoroughly. Dip the salmon escalopes one at a time in the flour mixture and set aside.
2. Heat butter in a sauté pan. When it stops foaming, add the salmon escalopes or fillets, cooking on one side just until the fish feels firm and is lightly browned; quickly turn over and lightly brown the second side for 30 seconds or so, until heated through.
3. Sprinkle with soy sauce and lemon juice. Garnish with the fresh cilantro or Italian parsley and serve immediately with the Nutted Wild Rice and the vegetables.

Nutted Wild Rice

Serves 6.

1 tsp.	salt
6 c.	water
1-1/2 c.	wild rice
7 Tbs.	butter
3/4 c.	coarsely chopped walnuts

1. Cook wild rice in simmering salted water for 20 to 30 minutes, or till cooked and water has evaporated.
2. Drain and mix with 4 Tbs. butter. Sauté walnuts in remaining butter for 3 to 5 minutes until golden brown.
3. Fold nuts into the rice and serve immediately.

"Learn to sense the flow."

— Ruth Montgomery

Julienne of Fresh, Braised Vegetables

Serves 6 to 8.

1/2 lb.	carrots
3/4 lb.	turnips
3/4 lb.	parsnips
1/2 lb.	green beans, washed and trimmed
	Salt and freshly ground black pepper to taste
1-1/2 Tbs.	fresh, minced dill
3 Tbs.	butter

1. Peel and julienne the carrots, turnips, and parsnips. If the beans are long, cut them in half. They should be about the same length as the other vegetables, give or take a half-inch or so.
2. Melt butter in a large skillet over moderate heat.
3. Add the carrots, turnips, and parsnips to the pan and season generously with salt and pepper to taste.
4. Toss the vegetables well in the butter. Cover the pan and cook on low heat for 10 minutes. Add the green beans and cook for 5 minutes longer, or until the vegetables are tender when pierced with knife.
5. Uncover, stir in dill, and adjust seasoning.

Pear and Pine Nut Cake

This is a comforting yet elegant, three-step dessert cake. Do start soaking the dried fruits the day before you intend to make this cake. The thick, rich crème fraiche is used a great deal in France with sweet and savory dishes alike. A tablespoon in a French vinaigrette to make it creamy is very nice. Also good on other desserts or baked fruits, or in sauces.

Serves 8 to 10.

A. Prepare the crème fraiche at least two days ahead.

Crème Fraiche:

2 c.	heavy cream
2 Tbs.	sour cream

1. Mix the two creams together well and place in a screw-top jar. Let stand on the counter for two days, until it is thick and congealed. May refrigerate after that for up to 10 days.

B. Soak the fruit a day ahead.

Fruit:

3 c.	water
2 heaping Tbs.	full-bodied black tea leaves
1/2 c.	sugar
6 oz.	dried pears
4 Tbs.	raisins

1. Bring water to a boil and pour over the tea leaves in a bowl; infuse for 5 minutes. Strain into another bowl and add the sugar, stirring until it dissolves.
2. Add the dried pears and raisins and leave to soak overnight. Drain the fruit.

"Value yourself at all times and in all circumstances."

— D.J.

C. Make the cake and assemble the dessert.

Cake:

1/2 c. + 2 Tbs. butter

     3/4 c.   sugar

        3   large eggs, separated

      1 c.   flour, sifted

    1 tsp.   baking powder, sifted

  1/4 tsp.   salt

    2 tsp.   grated lemon zest (yellow part only)

    4 Tbs.   pine nuts, lightly toasted in a dry sauté pan

              Powdered sugar, for dusting

1. Preheat oven to 350 degrees. Butter an 8- or 9-inch springform pan.
2. Cream butter and sugar together in a food processor. Add egg yolks one at a time, then the flour, baking powder, salt, and lemon zest. Remove batter to a large bowl.
3. Whisk the egg whites until they are stiff, and fold them in a third at a time into the mixture.
4. Mix in the soaked fruit and the toasted pine nuts. Transfer the mixture to the cake pan and bake for approximately 60 to 70 minutes, or until a skewer inserted into the cake comes out clean. Loosen the collar and leave to cool.
5. When cool, unmold cake onto a cake platter and dust lightly with powdered sugar. Serve with a dollop of crème fraiche or frozen yogurt, if you prefer.

Pacific Northwest Menu #5:

A Picnic at Washington Park

Tomato-Caper Bruschetta
Spicy Toasted Almonds
Herb Cheese and Crackers
Salad Nicoise
Fresh Green Grape Tart
Sangría

Dig out the candelabra for this picnic. It is worthy of it ... as are you, of course. How about picking a bunch of flowers or greens from your garden and just laying them on the blanket or picnic table as the centerpiece? Be sure to serve some good French baguette and butter with the salad for a hearty main course.

Take this picnic to a garden or a lake or a concert in the park — wherever you can enjoy nature. Go with your own passion, somewhere that moves you, and lifts and enhances your spirit as well.

Tomato-Caper Bruschetta

Makes 24 appetizers.

1 c.	firmly packed dried tomato slices (about 2 oz., found in wrapped packages in specialty stores or the gourmet aisle of your supermarket)
1 c.	boiling water
1	baguette
1	green onion, including top, coarsely chopped
1	clove garlic, peeled
1 Tbs.	drained capers
1 Tbs.	fresh oregano leaves
1-1/2 Tbs.	fresh lemon juice
1 Tbs.	balsamic vinegar
	Salt

1. In a small bowl, combine tomatoes with 1 cup boiling water; let stand until soft and pliable, about 15 minutes. Drain.
2. Cut baguette diagonally into 1/2-inch-thick slices. Arrange on a rimmed cookie sheet. Broil 4 to 6 inches from heat until toasted on each side, about 2 minutes total.
3. In the food processor, finely mince tomatoes, green onion, garlic, capers, and oregano with lemon juice and balsamic vinegar. Add salt to taste.
4. Spoon tomato mixture into a small bowl and accompany with toast. Spread tomato mixture onto toast and enjoy.

"The only thing you ever have any control of is your current thought."

— D.J.

Spicy Toasted Almonds

Makes 2 cups.

1-1/2 Tbs.	paprika
1 Tbs.	all-purpose flour
2 tsp.	garlic powder
1 tsp.	dill weed
1/2 tsp.	salt
1	large egg white
2 c.	whole, raw almonds

1. Preheat oven to 300 degrees. Spray a baking pan with nonstick cooking spray.
2. Combine paprika, flour, garlic powder, dill, and salt in a plastic bag. Set aside.
3. Beat egg white until frothy. Add almonds and toss to coat. Drain almonds on paper towels and then place in plastic bag with spices.
4. Tightly close bag and shake until almonds are well coated. Spread almonds in the prepared pan and bake 15 to 20 minutes, until a couple of the almonds start to split. Cool completely and store in an airtight container.

"The most powerful force in the world is love. The second most powerful force? The power of suggestion."

— John Boyle

Herb Cheese and Crackers

This cheese is great to take along in a small crock or bowl to spread on bread. Accompany it with fresh fruit and chilled white wine, or in this case, Sangría.

Makes about 1-1/2 cups.

8 oz.	cream cheese
1/2 c.	butter, softened (1 cube)
3/4 tsp.	thyme
1/2 tsp.	marjoram
1/8 tsp.	sage
2 tsp.	minced dried chives
1 tsp.	minced dried green onions
1/8 tsp.	beau monde seasoning
	Dash garlic powder

1. Mix all ingredients together in the food processor with steel blade. Taste for seasoning and add more herbs if you like. This is not an exacting kind of recipe, so taste as you go, and make notes for the next time you make it.
2. Wrap and let mellow in refrigerator for at least 24 hours.
3. Set cheese out to warm up before serving. Serve with crackers or bread rounds.

Salad Niçoise

This is my favorite main-course summer salad. It's easy to make and has everything in it as far as a balanced meal goes: fresh vegetables, potatoes for a starch, and high-protein eggs and fish. This salad has so much flavor and lots of textures — it is beautiful to look at and easy to assemble. And what a great presentation! You can put it right on a large platter and wrap it tightly with plastic to transport it, or take the marinated vegetables, tuna, eggs, lettuce, and vinaigrette in their own containers and fashion the salad "on sight" of the picnic. Lots of good, crusty French bread and butter are all you need as an accompaniment.

Serves 6 to 8.

Vinaigrette:

1 c.	extra-virgin olive oil
4 Tbs.	white wine vinegar
2 tsp.	Dijon mustard
1 tsp.	salt
	Freshly ground black pepper
1 Tbs.	your favorite herb: basil, tarragon, or oregano

Salad:

8	red potatoes, peeled, sliced, and boiled until tender
2 cans	white albacore tuna, packed in water
1/2 head	red leaf lettuce, or more
4	large, ripe tomatoes, quartered
1 lb.	fresh green beans, blanched al dente
4	hard-cooked large eggs, peeled and quartered
1	green pepper, cut into strips or rounds
1	yellow pepper, cut into strips or rounds
1 c.	black Kalamata olives, drained
1	large red onion, cut into rings
1 can	anchovy fillets, soaked in milk 30 minutes and then drained
1 Tbs.	minced fresh Italian parsley

1. Make the vinaigrette: Combine all ingredients in a screw-top jar.
2. Marinate the sliced potatoes in 3 Tbs. of the vinaigrette for 2 to 3 hours in the refrigerator.

3. Drain the water from the tuna.
4. Cover a large platter with washed, crisp salad greens. Arrange marinated potatoes, tomatoes, beans, and eggs around the platter. Mound the tuna in the center of the platter. Top with pepper strips and olives. Pour more of the vinaigrette evenly over all and garnish with the onion rings, anchovies, and minced parsley.

Fresh Green Grape Tart

I invented this tart prior to a picnic many years ago, and it was a big hit — a special surprise finish!

> 1   pie shell, baked and cooled

Custard Cream:
- 1 c.   sugar
- 5   large egg yolks
- 2/3 c.   sifted flour
- 2 c.   milk
- 1 tsp.   vanilla extract

Tart Topping:
-    Green, seedless grapes, halved, enough to cover the top of the whole pie
- 2 Tbs.   apricot brandy
- 1 c.   apricot preserves

1. Prepare the pie shell.
2. Make the custard: Gradually beat sugar into the egg yolks, and continue beating 2 to 3 minutes till mixture is pale yellow and forms a ribbon when the beaters are lifted. Beat in the flour.
3. In a heavy-bottomed saucepan, slowly bring milk to a boil; gradually add to egg mixture, beating constantly. Pour back into saucepan and cook over medium-high heat. Stir constantly but gently with a wire whip till thick and simmering.
4. Reduce heat to low and cook 2 to 3 minutes. If custard becomes lumpy, beat with electric mixer or put through a strainer and it will smooth right out. Remove from heat and cool, covered with wax paper. Press the wax paper right into the top of the custard. This prevents a skin from forming (plastic wrap also works.) Chill the custard well.
5. Spread the cold custard into the pie shell. Cover with the halved green grapes, rounded side up.
6. Melt the apricot preserves and add the apricot brandy. Strain mixture and paint the top of the grapes with the glaze.

"HUGS ... are practically perfect: They are low energy consumption, high energy yield, no monthly payments, nonfattening, inflation-proof, no pesticides, no preservatives, nontoxic, nonpolluting, and of course, fully returnable."

— Anonymous

Sangría

Serves 8 or more.

2 fifths	red Burgundy wine
1/2 c.	Cointreau or Triple Sec
3/4 c.	brandy
	Juice of 6 oranges
	Juice of 2 lemons
1 c.	sugar
2	oranges, sliced into rounds
1	lemon, sliced into rounds
1 pkg.	frozen Bing cherries (10-oz.)
2	fresh, ripe peaches, sliced, (or 1 [10-oz.] pkg. frozen)
	Chilled club soda to taste

1. In a large refrigerator container, combine the Burgundy, Cointreau, brandy, orange juice, lemon juice, and sugar. Chill several hours or overnight.
2. To serve, place the fruit slices into a large plastic juice container with a tight-fitting lid. Or, if you wish, you could take along a punch bowl and really do a number for this picnic.
3. Add chilled club soda to taste. I have several bottles on hand because, as you can see, this sangría is intense.

"You cannot hurry your life."

D.J.

Chapter Nine

Special Celebrations

I love the holidays. They seem to come along just as life becomes mundane or we need a lift to keep our spirits up. How appropriate! Whether it's Easter, Christmas, New Year's Eve, or the Fourth of July, holidays help us take a breather and enjoy family and friends without feeling guilty about not working or tending to the house and garden. People of all cultures invented holidays for just that purpose: to remember times past, to be happy, to share with others, and to add variety to our lives. And food plays such an integral part in big celebrations.

Whatever the occasion, be aware of the real reason for the celebration — love, sharing, connecting with others — in essence, spirit. This section contains menus that enhance that holiday feeling. The recipes are appropriate for any special party. Enjoy!

Special Celebration #1:

A Ringing in the New Year Buffet Dinner

Roasted Red Pepper Pâté
Pea Pods Stuffed with Boursin Cheese
Romaine Salad with Cashews and Oranges
Shrimp Curry with Rice and Condiments
Mango Mousse and Fresh Fruit

A buffet is much easier to put together than a sit-down dinner. It's so pleasant to have small tables of four scattered about, one or two of them in front of a fireplace with a crackling fire going, and perhaps another one where you might have a view. These features add much ambiance and are good for the spirit. Smaller tables make the party more intimate, even if you have a large number of people. I once sat one group of four up in my bedroom at a beautifully set, candlelit table, overlooking the lights of the city.

You might play musical chairs with each course, re-mixing guests, settings, and views. This raises the energy level and lets everyone reach a greater intimacy within the group. When the meal is over, have a group sing-along or game, bringing everyone together in a meeting of spirits, for a warm end to a great evening.

Roasted Red Pepper Pâté

Makes about 1-1/2 cups.

8 oz.	cream cheese, softened
1/3 c.	roasted red bell peppers
Dash	freshly ground black pepper
1 tsp.	minced garlic
2 cans	sliced, ripe olives, well drained (2.2-oz. can)
2 Tbs.	chopped fresh basil

Homemade crostini, or crackers

1. In food processor fitted with a steel blade, process cream cheese, bell peppers, garlic, and black pepper till blended and smooth.
2. Remove blade from processor and stir in olives and basil. Transfer to a serving dish and chill until firm.
3. Serve with crostini or crackers.

"My oneness with God and the universe constitutes my oneness with every spiritual idea, and that spiritual idea will express itself as home, friend, student, patient, book or teacher ... anything of which I have need."

— D.J.

Pea Pods Stuffed with Boursin Cheese

Serves 12 or more.

50 to 60	tender, young snow peas, cleaned and stems removed
8 oz.	cream cheese, softened
3 Tbs.	mayonnaise
1 tsp.	Dijon mustard
1 Tbs.	finely chopped fresh dill, or 1 tsp. dried
1	clove garlic, crushed
	Seasoning salt to taste

1. Blanch peas in boiling water for 30 seconds only. Plunge immediately into cold water to stop cooking and preserve their color.
2. With a sharp knife, slit open the straight seam of each snow pea.
3. Mix together remaining ingredients in food processor. Spoon into pastry bag.
4. Pipe into pea pods with a small tip. Chill before serving. Place decoratively on a serving platter.

Romain Salad with Cashews and Oranges

Serves 8.

3 heads	romaine lettuce, washed, dried, and torn into bite-size pieces
1 c.	salted cashews
1-1/2 c.	thinly sliced sweet red onion
2	large navel oranges, peeled and separated into segments

Dressing:

1/4 c.	cider vinegar
1 heaping Tbs.	Dijon mustard
	Salt and freshly ground black pepper
1/4 tsp.	ground cumin
Pinch	cardamom
2/3 c.	canola oil

1. Combine all salad ingredients in a large salad bowl.
2. Combine all dressing ingredients in a screw-top jar and shake well. Chill.
3. When ready to serve, add some dressing to salad and toss lightly. You probably will not need it all of the dressing, so add it sparingly. The ingredients should be just coated with the dressing and not at all soggy.

"Surrender is giving up control but not losing power: It does not mean giving up your power to another person. On the contrary, it is an act made to increase your own power."

— Anonymous

Shrimp Curry with Rice and Condiments

This is a simple English curry for American palates, a more subtle curry dish than most. It's very festive and a little exotic with all of the condiments. A nice departure from traditional holiday flavors. You may substitute 2 lbs. boned and skinned chicken breasts in place of the shrimp, since chicken is easier on the budget.

I let everyone help themselves to any curry and condiment combination that they like. Whenever I'm asked "How do we do this?" my answer is always "However you like" — on the top, on the side, in whatever combination appeals. I like everything sprinkled over the top, with just the chutney on the side. That's my way — let spirit be your guide!

Serves 8.

Sauce:

3 Tbs.	canola oil
1	large onion, diced
1	medium, tart apple, peeled, cored, and diced
3	cloves garlic, minced
3 Tbs.	flour
3 Tbs.	minced fresh Italian parsley
2-1/2 c.	chicken stock
1-3/4 c.	canned coconut milk
-1/2 Tbs.	tomato paste
3 Tbs.	creamy peanut butter

1. Place oil in a skillet over moderate heat. Sauté onion, apple, garlic, and parsley until tender but not brown.
2. Add flour and cook without browning, 2 to 3 minutes.
3. Whisk in chicken stock, coconut milk, tomato paste, and peanut butter, until mixture is smooth and well heated, but do not boil. Add a little more chicken stock if the sauce becomes too thick.

Spice Mixture:

1-1/2 Tbs.	canola oil
2 Tbs.	curry powder
1 tsp.	ground coriander
1 Tbs.	fresh, minced ginger
1 1/2 tsp.	ground cumin
3/4 tsp.	cinnamon
1-1/2 tsp.	salt

My Way:

Basic Cooked Rice to serve 8:

2 c. long-grain rice
4 c. water
1-1/2 tsp. salt

1. Place the water and salt into a 4-quart sauce pan and bring to the boil.

2. Add the rice, stir once around with a fork, turn heat to simmer, and cook, covered, for about 20 to 30 minutes, or until all of the liquid is absorbed and the rice is nice and fluffy.

1. Place oil in skillet over low heat.
2. Add curry powder, ground coriander, ginger, cumin, and cinnamon and sauté for 2 to 4 minutes. Blend in the salt.

Shrimp Curry and Condiments:

    2 lbs.   raw shrimp, shelled and deveined
    3 Tbs.   butter

Toasted coconut, roasted salted peanuts, chutney, chopped green onions, cucumber, tomato, green pepper, red pepper, hard-boiled eggs, bananas, pineapple, mango, Kiwi, and chopped fresh parsley, as condiments

1. Sauté shrimp in butter just until pink, 3 to 4 minutes at most.
2. Pour spice mixture into the sauce and blend in until smooth. Simmer gently on low heat for 10 minutes.
3. Add the sautéed shrimp. Taste for seasoning. Serve over the rice (see "My Way," below) and serve the condiments on the side.

"I thank Spirit for new and old relationships."

— D.J.

Mango Mousse and Fresh Fruit

This dessert comes from Richard Plainfield of the wonderful, East Indian Plainfield's Mayur Restaurant in Portland, Oregon — thank you Richard and Rhaika! It's wonderful, rich, and easy to make.

Serves 10 to 12.

1/2 can	mango purée (purchased from an East Indian market) (#2 can)
2 c.	heavy cream
1 (8-oz.) can	sweetened, condensed milk
1/2 c.	whole milk
3/4 tsp.	powdered cardamom

1. Place the mango purée into the bowl of a food processor. Slowly add the heavy cream, sweetened, condensed milk, whole milk, and cardamom. Blend well.
2. Spray 10 or 12 small paper drinking cups with nonstick cooking spray. Pour the mango mixture into the cups and freeze overnight. Keeps well in freezer for 2 months. After they are frozen, place them in a double plastic bag and seal tightly. Serve frozen with fresh tropical fruit slices.

*

Special Celebration Menu #2:

A Springtime Easter Brunch

Pineapple Vodka
White Sangría
Cheddar Sausage Puffs with Spicy Mustard Sauce
Coulibiac of Salmon
Spinach Timbales
Poached Pears Curaçao

This menu is a good example of the global blending of recipes into a menu in which each dish is compatible with the other. Here I have blended Russian, Spanish, American, and French recipes to form a delicious Easter or spring celebration brunch. I first tasted Coulibiac in a grand, old hotel in Leningrad. The dining room atmosphere was very Old Russian, with a string quartet playing classical music. The mood was adventurous and romantic at the same time, and filled me with an excitement to explore this interesting and beautiful city of bridges. The biggest lesson I learned while in what was then the Soviet Union was that people all over the world are far more similar than different. I realized that no matter our nationality, we all have the same needs, wants, and desires as human beings. I wondered what the Cold War was all about.

Pineapple Vodka

I really like this drink chilled and made with good Russian vodka. If you serve it strained, serve it in a martini glass with a small wedge or sliver of the pineapple alongside. Or serve it in a wine glass large enough to fit a wedge of the pineapple inside. Delicious and unusual!

Serves 8 or more.

1	medium, ripe pineapple
1 fifth	vodka (24 oz.)

1. Remove top and bottom of pineapple. Immerse pineapple in cold water for 15 minutes. Drain and slice pineapple into 1-inch-thick rounds. Cut each slice in half.
2. Combine pineapple halves and vodka in a 2-1/2 — quart glass or ceramic jar, bowl, or pitcher.
3. Cover tightly and let stand at room temperature for three days.
4. Strain the vodka into a smaller pitcher. Serve at room temperature or chill, tightly covered, in freezer for several hours before serving in fruit-garnished glasses.

"With Spirit as my guide, all things are possible. I welcome the blessings of a creative imagination into my mind and into my life."
— Anonymous

White Sangría

A friend of mine served the usual red sangria at her daughter's wedding, which she held in her home. Unfortunately several spills occurred, which ruined the white carpeting that runs throughout her beautiful house. White sangría alleviates that problem; it is also lighter than the red and still has very good, fresh, fruit flavor.

Serves 6.

1/3 c.	fresh lemon juice
1/3 c.	fresh lime juice
1 c.	fresh orange juice
1 c.	club soda
1-1/2 c.	ginger ale
1 fifth	dry white wine, chilled (24 oz.)
1/2 c.	Pimm's Cup (purchased at the liquor store)
1	naval orange, cut into wedges
1	lemon, cut into wedges

Ice cubes

1. In a large pitcher stir together citrus juices, club soda, ginger ale, wine, Pimm's Cup, and half of the orange and lemon wedges.
2. Add ice cubes, and serve sangría with remaining orange and lemon wedges.

Cheddar Sausage Puffs with Spicy Mustard Sauce

Start the mustard sauce the day before you make these savory appetizers.

Makes 48 puffs.

Spicy Mustard Sauce:

1/3 to 1/2 c.	dry mustard
1/2 c.	white vinegar
1/2 c.	sugar
1	large egg yolk

1. Combine dry mustard and vinegar in a small bowl. Start with 1/3 cup of the mustard and then if the sauce is too thin, add the rest of it. Cover and let stand at room temperature overnight.
2. The following day, combine mustard mixture, sugar, and egg yolk in a small saucepan. Simmer over low heat till slightly thickened. Cover and store in refrigerator up to one month. Serve at room temperature. Makes about 1-1/3 cup.

Puffs:

12 oz.	spicy bulk pork sausage
1 lb.	sharp Cheddar cheese, shredded
1 c.	buttermilk biscuit mix

1. Preheat oven to 350 degrees. In a medium bowl, mix sausage, cheese and biscuit mix until blended.
2. Shape into walnut-size balls. Place on a rack in a shallow pan. Bake 35 to 45 minutes or until lightly browned. Serve immediately with the mustard sauce. May cool and freeze puffs; thaw frozen puffs 1 to 2 hours and bake as above.

"I discover the comfort and peace of mind I seek by giving my full attention and respect to my Spirit."

— D.J.

Coulibiac of Salmon

This dish originated in Russia, and means "a hot fish pie." Beautifully suited to salmon, it is truly spectacular to serve and as great tasting as it looks. True, it makes a very rich meal, but once in a while it's good to indulge your spirit. The recipe is not so difficult as it is time-consuming. Prepare it only for people who truly appreciate such a work of art. In my opinion, this is the best leftover in the world (if there's any left!) You need to make the dough the day before you plan to serve the Coulibiac. Serve it on a big silver platter, decorated with lemon slices and parsley sprigs. Let your guests see it whole — they will "ooh and ahh" over the whole presentation.

Makes enough dough and filling for one Coulibiac, plus dough for approximately fifteen 4-inch brioche rolls. Serves 12.

A. Begin the brioche dough.

Brioche Dough:

2 tsp.	sugar
2 pkgs.	active dry yeast
1/2 c.	warm water
1/3 c.	butter
1/3 c.	sugar
1-1/4 tsp.	salt
1 c.	milk
6	large whole eggs, at room temperature
2	large egg yolks, at room temperature
6-1/2 c.	flour

1. Mix 2 tsp. sugar, the yeast, and the warm water; let stand 5 minutes.
2. Heat milk to warm. Mix butter, sugar, and salt until creamy; add yeast mixture, milk, egg yolks and whole eggs. Add flour gradually and beat well for 10 minutes. This is best done in a mixer with a dough hook.
3. Cover and let rise in a warm place 2 hours or until double in bulk.
4. Punch down and beat with wooden spoon. Place in a large, greased bowl; cover and refrigerate 6 to 8 hours or longer. Meanwhile, prepare the rice filling as follows.

B. Prepare the rice filling.

Rice Filling:

1-1/2 c.	chicken stock
2 tsp.	fresh lemon juice
2 tsp.	lemon zest
3/4 tsp.	salt
3/4 c.	uncooked, long-grain white rice
2 Tbs.	chopped fresh Italian parsley

1. Place all ingredients except the rice and parsley in a pot and bring to boil. Add the rice, stirring once with a fork. Turn heat down to simmer and cook the rice, covered, for about 20 to 25 minutes, or till all of the liquid is absorbed. 2. Fold in the parsley after the rice is cooked. You may make this filling in advance if you wish. Prepare the following sauce and mix the rice into it.

C. Make the sauce for the rice filling.

Sauce:

2-1/2	Tbs. butter
2-1/2 Tbs.	Wondra "instant" flour (superior in sauces to all-purpose flour, as it does not "lump up")
	Salt and freshly ground black pepper
	Grated nutmeg to taste
1 Tbs.	chopped fresh Italian parsley
1 c.	milk
2 Tbs.	heavy cream
2	large eggs yolks, lightly beaten
1/2 c.	grated Gruyère cheese
3 Tbs.	Crème Fraiche (see recipe for Pear and Pine Nut Cake, in the Pacific Northwest section of this book.)

1. Melt butter, add flour, and cook 2 minutes. Stir in salt, pepper, nutmeg, and parsley.
2. Slowly add milk and cream and cook until thick, whisking constantly to make a smooth sauce.
3. Stir some of the hot mixture into the beaten egg yolks, and beat briskly so the eggs don't curdle. Return yoke mixture to the sauce, stirring, and sprinkle in the cheese. Stir in the crème fraiche.
4. Fold the sauce into the rice and refrigerate it until ready to complete the coulibiac.

D. Make the salmon filling and complete the dish.

Remainder:

1/2 lb.	white mushrooms, cleaned and sliced
1/3 c.	clarified butter, for sautéing (see "My Way")
4	hard-cooked, large eggs, peeled, and sliced
1-1/2 lbs.	raw shrimp, shelled, deveined, rinsed in cold water, and drained
	Salt to taste
	Freshly ground black pepper to taste
1 to 2 c.	flour
1 1b.	salmon fillets, cut into 3-inch-square pieces
1 Tbs.	fresh lemon juice
1	large egg white, lightly beaten

Lemon Butter:

3/4 c.	butter (1-1/2 cubes)
2 Tbs.	fresh lemon juice
1 Tbs.	lemon zest

Lemon slices, for garnish

Fresh Italian parsley sprigs, for garnish

1. Sauté mushrooms in a little of the clarified butter and add to the rice. Slices eggs and set aside.
2. Add butter if needed. Sauté shrimp, salt lightly, and then cut in half lengthwise. Set aside.
3. Season flour with salt and pepper to taste. Dip salmon into seasoned flour and sauté briefly in a little more butter until golden brown, 2 to 3 minutes per side. Set aside.
4. Turn out the dough on a floured board and knead lightly. Cut off 1/3 of dough and save to make brioche rolls.
5. Of the remaining 2/3 of the dough, remove a small piece the size of your fist to use for decorations.
6. Cut the rest of the dough in half, and roll each of the halves into a 10x16-inch rectangle.
7. Drape one rectangle over the rolling pin and place it on a rimless, greased, nonstick baking sheet. However, be careful so that the baked coulibiac does not slide off the pan when you take it out of the oven. The rimless baking sheet will allow the coulibiac to be easily transferred to a large serving platter.

My Way:

Clarified Butter:

1. Melt 1/2 c. butter in a saucepan.

2. Skim off the foamy substance that rises to the top, and discard.

3. Pour the remaining butter into a bowl, discarding the milky solids at the bottom of the pan (whey). Clarified butter keeps longer than fresh, and does not burn as easily when heated.

8. Spread half of the rice filling on the pastry, top with layers of salmon, shrimp, and hard-cooked eggs. Do not place filling right to the edge of the pastry; leave a border of about 1-1/2 inches all the way around.
9. Sprinkle with lemon juice, and add the rest of the rice.
10. Brush border with some of the beaten egg white. Cover everything with the second pastry rectangle. Seal edges and decorate edges with a fork or your fingers to form a rope pattern.
11. Roll out ball of dough for decorations and cut out leaves, flowers, fish shapes or just rectangular strips.
12. Brush entire coulibiac with the egg white, and decorate the top and sides of it as well. Cover with a clean kitchen towel and let rest in a warm place 25 minutes. Preheat oven to 350 degrees.
13. Bake coulibiac for 25 minutes. When nearly done, place all of the lemon butter ingredients in a bowl and melt in the microwave just prior to serving. Serve coulibiac immediately with hot lemon butter.

Spinach Timbales

The timbales go very well with the Coulibiac of Salmon, not only in flavor but as an elegant garnish.

Serves 8.

1/2 c.	chopped onion
1/4 c.	butter (1/2 cube)
3 c.	fresh spinach, cooked and drained well
1 c.	light cream
	Salt and freshly ground black pepper to taste
1/4 tsp.	freshly grated nutmeg
1/2 tsp.	thyme or basil
2	large whole eggs
2	large egg yolks
3	ripe tomatoes, thinly sliced
2	hard-cooked large eggs, finely chopped, or grated lemon zest, for garnish

1. Preheat oven to 325 degrees. In skillet on stovetop, sauté onion in butter over medium heat until tender. Add spinach and cook a minute or more. Add cream, and cook until cream has evaporated. Remove from heat.
2. Season with salt, pepper, nutmeg, and herbs.
3. Beat eggs and yolks well and blend into the spinach mixture. Spray eight 6-oz. timbale molds with nonstick cooking spray, and place spinach mixture into the molds.
4. Set in a large baking pan, and pour in enough hot water to reach 2/3 of the way up the sides of the molds. (This keeps them nice and moist when cooked.) Bake for 25 minutes or till set.
5. Let stand 5 minutes, then turn out and serve by inverting each timbale onto a slice of tomato and topping each with a bit of hard-cooked egg or grated lemon zest.

"If you do not love yourself totally, wholly, and fully somewhere along the way you learned not to. You can unlearn it. Start being kind to yourself now."
— Louise Hay

Poached Pears Curaçao

This dessert is a perfect, simple finish to any winter menu — whether a holiday or not.

Serves 6 to 10, depending on how many will want a half or a whole pear. After this meal, half is probably enough.

1-1/2 c.	sugar
1 length	vanilla bean (3-inch)
3 c.	water
1/2	lemon, quartered
6	winter pears, peeled, sliced in half lengthwise and cored
2	oranges
1/2 c.	fresh orange juice
1/2 c. + 3 Tbs.	red currant jelly, divided
3 Tbs.	orange Curaçao
1 c.	heavy cream
3 Tbs.	powdered sugar
1 tsp.	vanilla extract

"Give thanks for the abundance in your life."
— D.J.

1. In a large Dutch oven or other deep, heavy pot, combine sugar, vanilla bean, and water. Add lemon quarters and simmer syrup 5 minutes, until sugar dissolves.
2. Add the pears and simmer in syrup 10 to 15 minutes or just till tender but NOT falling apart.
3. Meanwhile, remove orange zest (orange part only) with a sharp paring knife, in the longest strips possible. Julienne these strips, and reserve enough to garnish the whipped cream later. Drop the remaining orange zest into a small pot of boiling water and cook 10 minutes. Drain and reserve zest, discarding cooking water.
4. When pears are done, remove them to a clear, glass serving bowl, and sprinkle them with the cooked orange strips.
5. Add orange juice and currant jelly to pear liquid. Let jelly melt over medium heat and reduce this syrup until it is thick enough to coat a spoon.
6. Add the Curaçao, blend, and pour syrup over the pears.
7. Whip heavy cream, adding powdered sugar, until it holds soft peaks. Add vanilla and whip just to blend.
8. Place whipped cream in a small serving bowl with a few reserved orange strips on top for garnish, and pass at the table to serve over the pears.

Special Celebration #3:

A Thanksgiving Dinner

Peppered Pecans
Pumpkin Soup in a Pumpkin
Stuffed Loin of Pork with Madeira Sauce
Vegetable Tarts
Garlic Baked Potato Wedges
English Trifle Tropicale

This is not the usual traditional Thanksgiving feast, I know, but an elegant departure if spirit says you need a change. Part of growth and the capacity for joy is being flexible and welcoming change, in the food that we eat as well as in other areas of our lives. When we do things the same way over and over, our lives become stale and we begin to take things for granted. Small exercises like preparing new recipes and trying different menus bring us a greater zest for living and let our spirits shine through. A great deal of this out-of-the-ordinary menu can be made ahead.

Peppered Pecans

These are great to have on hand as a quick, simple hors d'oeuvre with cocktails. Keep them in the refrigerator to insure freshness, but bring them out of the refrigerator 1 hour before they are served.

Makes 2 lbs.

2 lbs.	shelled pecan halves
1/2 c.	butter
1-1/2 tsp.	Tabasco sauce
1 tsp.	salt
1-1/2 tsp.	dried thyme
1-1/2 tsp.	dried marjoram
1-1/2 tsp.	dried rosemary
1-1/2 tsp.	dried oregano
2-1/2 tsp.	freshly cracked black pepper

1. Preheat oven to 300 degrees.
2. Spread pecans on 2 baking sheets.
3. Melt the butter with the Tabasco and the salt; pour over the pecans.
4. Sprinkle with herbs and pepper and mix well with a rubber spatula.
5. Bake for 45 minutes, stirring occasionally. Cool at room temperature. Serve as a salad garnish or as an appetizer with drinks.

"Simplify."
— Henry David Thoreau

Pumpkin Soup in a Pumpkin

The pumpkins that we use for carving jack-o-lanterns are tasteless and therefore not good for cooking with. Nowadays, at least in large cities, there are so many varieties of pumpkins in markets; ask your green grocer what she/he would recommend. The best by far are French pumpkins — they have a nice buttery, full-bodied flavor that makes this soup special. If you cannot find a decent pumpkin, use yams instead. That's what all of the canned pumpkin is made from.

Serving this soup in a hollowed-out pumpkin makes a beautiful presentation — a reminder of the abundance our planet provides.

Serves 8 as a first course.

2	small French pumpkins, seeds removed (one that will yield at least 4 c. of pulp for cooking, and one hollowed out for use as a tureen) Salted water, for cooking pumpkin cubes
2 Tbs.	butter
2 c.	chopped onion
2	shallots, minced
2	cloves garlic, minced
6 c.	chicken stock
1-1/2	tsp. salt
3/4	tsp. thyme
7	white peppercorns (buy in bulk, if possible)
1/2 c.	heavy cream, or light cream if you must
2 Tbs.	minced fresh Italian parsley Freshly grated nutmeg

1. Preheat oven to 375 degrees. Cut one of the pumpkins into 3 or 4 pieces; then peel and seed it. Cut prepared pieces into 1-inch chunks. (You should have about 4 c. of pulp chunks.) On stovetop in a saucepan, bring salted water to a boil, reduce heat, and cook the pumpkin cubes till tender. Drain and set aside.

2. Melt the butter in a large, heavy pot and sauté onion, shallots, and garlic for 5 minutes on medium heat, till soft but not brown.

3. Add 3 c. of the cooked pumpkin cubes (set aside remaining 1 cup), The chicken stock, salt, thyme, and white peppercorns. Simmer 20 minutes.

4. In the meantime, bake the pumpkin "tureen" in the preheated oven for 20 to 30 minutes.
5. Purée the soup in a blender and return to the soup pot.
6. Add the cream, taste for seasoning, and just heat through.
7. Remove the baked pumpkin tureen to a platter and fill with the hot pumpkin soup.
8. Add the remaining 1 c. of pumpkin cubes to the soup. Garnish with the nutmeg and parsley.

Stuffed Loin of Pork with Madeira Sauce

This is a very special way of preparing a loin of pork. I choose and create recipes that have ingredients that I like, are different, and of course taste delicious. This particular variety of ingredients combine beautifully with the Madeira wine to make a delicious sauce to accompany the pork slices. The stuffing has great color, with the green basil and pistachios and the orange carrots. This grand dish looks very festive indeed — a great addition to your visual feast.

Serves 10 to 12.

3	large cloves garlic, minced
2 c.	fresh basil leaves, coarsely chopped
1/2 c.	coarsely chopped pistachio nuts, lightly toasted
1/4 c.	golden raisins
1	large egg, beaten
1	pork loin, butterflied (3-lb.)
1	large carrot, thinly sliced
1	large stalk celery, thinly sliced
2-1/2 Tbs.	fat from roasting pan
2 Tbs.	flour
2 c.	chicken stock
3/4 c.	water
1/2 c.	Madeira
	Salt to taste

"Any spiritual message is the Grace of God reaching human consciousness."
— Anonymous

1. Preheat oven to 425 degrees. Make stuffing: Combine the first 5 ingredients.
2. Place meat, fat side down, on your work surface and spread with the stuffing.
3. Roll and tie securely at 1/2-inch intervals.
4. Place vegetables in the bottom of the roasting pan. Place the stuffed meat on the vegetable bed and roast 15 minutes at 425 degrees.
5. Reduce heat to 375 degrees and continue to roast for 45 minutes more.
6. Remove roast to a serving tray and keep warm, covered with foil.
7. Pour off all but about 2-1/2 Tbs. of the pan drippings, add flour, and cook on stovetop, stirring, for 2 to 3 minutes. Add chicken stock and water to the pan. Bring to simmer, stirring up all of the brown bits (they add lots of flavor.)

8.   Strain the sauce, pressing down hard on the vegetables to extract all of the juice. Return sauce to pan.

9.   Add the Madeira and stir. Raise heat to medium-high and cook sauce 20 minutes, whisking frequently until it coats a spoon. Add salt to taste and 2 more Tbs. Madeira.

10.   Slice the stuffed pork 1/4- to 1/2-inch thick. Pour sauce into a sauce boat and serve all immediately.

Vegetable Tarts

These tarts are a nice departure from plain, cooked vegetables and can be made ahead up to the assembly steps, which should be done just before baking and serving. They are delicious and great with any holiday meal, especially any roasted meats or chicken.

Serves 6 to 8.

A. Make and prebake the tart pastry.

Pastry:

2-1/2 c.	flour
1 c.	Crisco vegetable shortening
3/4 tsp.	salt
1/3 c.	ice water
1/2 tsp.	cider vinegar
1	large egg yolk

1. Cut together flour, Crisco, and salt. Mix ice water, vinegar, and egg yolk together. Add to flour mixture and blend with a fork just until the dough holds together.
2. Pull it all together with your hands and place on a piece of plastic wrap. Wrap up and chill the dough for an hour or longer.
3. Preheat oven to 425 degrees. Bring pastry dough to room temperature for about 30 minutes, and then roll out to desired size. Line desired tart pans or baking dishes with pastry.
4. Prick pastry all over with a fork, cover with foil, and bake for 10 minutes. Remove foil and bake 5 minutes more.

B. Prepare the vegetables and fill the tarts.

Vegetables:

2	medium carrots
12	small boiling onions
1/3 head	cauliflower, cleaned
1 c.	frozen peas, thawed and drained
6 to 8	large mushrooms
	Butter, for sautéing

1. Scrape and thickly slice the carrots. Peel onions. Break cauliflower into 12 small flowerettes.
2. Bring a saucepan of water to a boil and drop in carrots, onions, and peas; cook for 4 minutes. Add cauliflower.
3. Cook 4 to 5 minutes longer. Drain and let cool a few minutes. Divide the vegetables among the tart shells.
4. Clean whole mushrooms and sauté in butter 4 to 5 minutes. Place one mushroom in center of each tart.

C. Make the sauce, and assemble and finish baking the tarts.

Sauce Aurora:

3 Tbs.	butter
2	cloves garlic, crushed
1/2	onion, minced
3 Tbs.	flour
2-1/2 c.	hot milk
5	black peppercorns
1/2 tsp.	thyme
2	bay leaves
	Salt
	Grated nutmeg
2-1/2 Tbs.	tomato paste
2 Tbs.	red wine
1/2 tsp.	dried, crushed marjoram, or 1 Tbs. fresh

1. Preheat oven to 375 degrees. In saucepan on stovetop, heat butter over moderate heat until bubbly. Add garlic and stir for 1 to 2 minutes.
2. Add onion and cook over low heat for 3 to 4 minutes.
3. Stir in flour and continue cooking 2 to 3 minutes.
4. Remove from heat, add milk, and whisk until smooth. Return to heat and add peppercorns, thyme, bay leaves, salt, and nutmeg. Cook for 10 to 15 minutes till thick.
5. Strain sauce through a sieve. Add tomato paste, red wine, and the marjoram.
6. Stir with whisk and heat through. Pour over the vegetable tarts and bake 15 to 20 minutes. If not baking right away, keep sauce warm and then pour over vegetables just before baking.

"Dreams are the seedlings of realities."
— James Allen

Garlic Baked Potato Wedges

These are easy to make and are great alongside any roasted meats, especially barbecued meats. There are never any leftovers.

Serves 6 to 8.

3 lbs.	medium to large red potatoes, scrubbed well and cut into bite-sized wedges
1/4 c.	butter, or 4 Tbs. canola oil
5	cloves garlic, crushed
1-1/2 tsp.	salt
	Freshly ground black pepper to taste
	Chopped fresh Italian parsley

1. Preheat oven to 400 degrees. Place potatoes into an oven-proof baking dish.
2. Melt butter and add the crushed garlic cloves to it, stirring well.
3. Pour garlic butter over the potatoes and season with salt and pepper.
4. Bake for 50 to 60 minutes or till tender inside, crispy outside, and golden brown.
5. Garnish with parsley and serve immediately.

English Trifle Tropicale

This dessert comes from England originally. The English usually had most of these ingredients on hand, so to make up a quick dessert, it was a "trifle" of this and a "trifle" of that, hence the name, "English Trifle." Of course, usually it is made with fresh berries, but in wintertime they are hard to come by, so I have created a trifle with tropical fruits. Tropical fantasy is always appealing to me at Christmas time, especially when it's cold and snowy out. This can be made up to a day ahead. It's elegant and delicious!

Serves 10.

2 c.	vanilla custard (prepare 1 large pkg. Jello instant vanilla pudding mix)
1	frozen Sara Lee pound cake (12-oz.)
8 oz.	pineapple jam
1 c.	medium dry sherry
1/4 c.	brandy
2 c.	heavy cream
2 Tbs.	powdered sugar
3 to 4 c.	mixed fruit, such as kiwi, pineapple, bananas, oranges, and star fruit
1 c.	slivered almonds, toasted

1. Make the custard according to package directions and chill until thick.
2. Slice pound cake into 1/2-inch-thick slices. Spread the slices with the jam and place them in the bottom of a deep, clear glass bowl.
3. Sprinkle the cake with the sherry and the brandy and set aside.
4. Whip the cream and, as it thickens, slowly add the powdered sugar.
5. Keep some of the fruit aside for garnish and place the rest of it over the cake and liquor. Pour the custard over all.
6. Pipe or pour the whipped cream over the custard.
7. Garnish with the remaining fruits and the toasted, slivered almonds.
8. Chill up to 5 hours or till ready to serve.

My Way:

Place some of the Kiwi slices around the sides of the trifle bowl and pushed about halfway down into the dessert so they stay upright. This makes for a smashing visual impact when served.

Special Celebration Menu #4:

A Feast for All Celebrations

Crisp Vegetable with Watercress Dip
Lobster Bisque
Baked Red Snapper Dijon
Saffron Rice
Bûche de Noël

Here's a blended dinner of many cultures to celebrate holidays that will leave rich memories for years to come. You may enjoy this meal year-round of course, but I like to prepare it for a special celebration of togetherness, forgiveness, and joy. You may have other ideas and meanings from which to build your own traditions, so please add your own desires to this diverse meal.

Crisp Vegetable with Watercress Dip

Arrange the prepared vegetables of your choice in a beautiful basket lined with a crisp, white, cloth napkin — this really sets off the color of the vegetables. An artistic visual presentation shows care, beauty, and respect for the ingredients. Food really does taste better when served in a beautiful way. In choosing and preparing these fresh vegetables, as is so important in cooking with spirit — taste, taste, taste!

Dip serves 6 to 8; double or triple as necessary.

Your choice of vegetables:

Fresh:

Artichoke Hearts	Green Onions
Bell Peppers	Hearts of Palm
Broccoli	Jicama
Carrots	Mushrooms
Cauliflower	Radishes
Celery	Tomatoes
Cucumber	Zucchini
Fennel	

Cooked:

Asparagus	Green Beans
Tiny Red Potatoes	

1. Clean and cut all raw vegetables into serving-size pieces.
2. Boil the potatoes in salted water until just tender. Cook the green beans and asparagus lightly in a steamer basket to take away the bitter taste they sometimes have when raw, although I have tasted some in season that do not need cooking at all. Serve with dip.

Watercress Dip:

1-1/2 c.	loosely packed watercress, leaves only
1/3	fresh basil leaves, coarsely chopped
1	clove garlic
1/4 c.	extra-virgin olive oil
1/2 c.	finely grated Parmesan cheese
1/3 c.	light cream
1/4 c.	ground pecans
1 Tbs.	minced fresh Italian parsley

My Way:

The reason for bringing this dip and similar complex dishes to room temperature before serving is that when foods are warm, subtle flavors are enhanced. They are more intense than when the dish is cold.

Freshly ground black pepper
Salt to taste

1. Place watercress, basil, garlic, and oil in food processor. Process to a fine purée.
2. Transfer mixture to medium bowl. Stir in Parmesan cheese, cream, pecans, parsley, and pepper to taste. Blend thoroughly and refrigerate, covered, 1 to 2 hours to blend flavors.
3. Remove from refrigerator 45 minutes before serving. Taste for seasoning, adding salt if necessary. Transfer to a serving bowl. Makes about 2 cups.

Lobster Bisque

The difference between a creamed soup and a bisque is the use of milk in the base of the soup. This soup is delicious and very rich, so serve it with a lighter main course.

Serves 8 to 10.

2/3 c.	butter
1-1/2 lbs.	small, frozen lobster tails, cut into 2 to 3 pieces in their shell
2	medium carrots, peeled and diced
2 c.	chopped onions
3 sprigs	fresh Italian parsley
1	bay leaf
1/4 tsp.	thyme
1/2 c.	dry white wine
4 Tbs.	brandy, divided
6 c.	chicken stock (1-1/2 qts.)
1/4 c.	tomato paste
3/4 c.	flour
2 c.	light cream
1 qt.	milk (2% fat)
1 tsp.	salt, or to taste
1/4 tsp.	white pepper

1. Melt 2 Tbs. butter in a large heavy pot. Add the lobster pieces. Sauté, stirring occasionally, about 5 minutes or until the shells turn red.
2. Add vegetables and herbs. Cook until vegetables are tender.
3. Add the wine and 2 Tbs. of the brandy. Cook 1 minute.
4. Add chicken broth and tomato paste. Bring to a boil and simmer 8 to 10 minutes.
5. Remove lobster pieces with slotted spoon. Cool and remove meat from the shells.
6. Dice the lobster meat and reserve.
7. Melt remaining butter in saucepan over medium heat. Stir in the flour. Cook 1 minute, stirring constantly.
8. Add cream, milk, salt, and pepper. Bring just to a boil, stirring constantly. Turn heat down and simmer 5 minutes.

"There is no us and them — we are all one."

— D.J.

9.   Mix the flour/milk mixture with the broth mixture and the lobster shells. Simmer for 30 minutes. Strain and discard all but the bisque. Add the lobster meat and 2 Tbs. brandy. Serve with toasted rye rounds.

Toasted Rye Rounds:
Rye bread cocktail rounds
Butter
Seasoning salt
Freshly grated Parmesan cheese

1.   Sprinkle buttered rye bread cocktail rounds with seasoning salt and grated Parmesan cheese.
2.   Broil until golden brown, 2 to 3 minutes.

Baked Red Snapper Dijon

Serves 6.

	Canola oil, for sautéing
6	fillets of red snapper
	Salt and freshly ground black pepper to taste
	Flour, enough to coat fish
5 Tbs.	butter
2	cloves garlic
1 c.	toasted bread crumbs
2 Tbs.	minced fresh Italian parsley
1/3 tsp.	thyme
2-1/2 Tbs.	Dijon mustard

Lemon wedges

1. Preheat oven to 350 degrees. Heat a small amount of oil in a skillet. Salt and pepper snapper fillets and coat with flour.
2. Sauté fillets only briefly, to seal in the juices. Remove to a flat baking pan.
3. Heat skillet and melt 5 Tbs. butter. Mash garlic and cook gently 1 minute. Add bread crumbs and toss to coat well. Add parsley and thyme and toss again.
4. Spread about 3/4 tsp. Dijon mustard on each fillet. Top with garlic-buttered crumbs. Bake for about 20 minutes. Serve each fillet with a lemon wedge on the side.

"If a man does not keep pace with his companions, perhaps it is because he hears a different drummer. Let him step to the music which he hears, however measured or far away."
— Henry David Thoreau

Saffron Rice

Serves 6 to 8.

3 c.	chicken stock
1/4 tsp.	saffron
1 tsp.	salt
1-1/2 c.	uncooked long-grain rice
1/2 c.	minced fresh Italian parsley
2 Tbs.	butter

1. Bring stock to boil. Add saffron and salt. Add rice and turn to low heat. Simmer for 25 minutes, until all liquid has been absorbed.
2. Add parsley and butter to rice, fluff, and serve hot with the red snapper.

Bûche de Noël (Chocolate Yule Log)

This is a classic French Christmas dessert that I love because it really connotes the holidays — and besides, it's chocolate! The history of the Yule log comes from Europe when many, many years ago the custom was to bring a real log for the fire as a gift when visiting family and friends. Somewhere along the way, the custom moved into the kitchen and evolved into a chocolate log. I have given this as a Christmas gift to friends because it is so special and is a labor of love.

Serves 10 to 12.

A. Make the cake base.

Cake:

6	large eggs, separated
1/2 tsp.	cream of tartar
1 c.	sugar
4 Tbs.	cocoa
4 Tbs.	flour
1/4 tsp.	salt
1 tsp.	vanilla extract

1. Separate the eggs while cold and let stand at room temperature for at least 1 hour.
2. Preheat oven to 325 degrees. In a warm, dry bowl, beat the 6 egg whites with the cream of tartar until frothy.
3. When the egg whites are frothy, slowly add 1/2 c. of the sugar, 1 Tbs. at a time. Continue beating the egg whites until they hold shiny, stiff peaks but are not dry.
4. Beat the egg yolks in another bowl, slowly adding the other 1/2 c. of sugar until mixture is light lemon yellow in color and thick.
5. Sift the sugar, cocoa, flour, and salt over the beaten yolks and beat until blended. Stir in the vanilla.
6. Stir 1/3 of the egg whites into the yolk mixture thoroughly. (This lightens the whole mixture, so it can easily be folded into the rest of the whites without overmixing.)
7. Carefully fold the remaining whites into the yolk mixture until just mixed in. (Do not overmix, or you will knock the air out of the whites, and the cake will not rise as much as it should while baking. Then, when it recedes, it will be tough and heavy instead of light in consistency.)

8.   Grease and line a jelly-roll pan with waxed paper, and grease and flour the waxed paper.

9.   Pour the cake batter carefully into the prepared pan, smoothing out the batter gently, and bake the cake for about 20 to 30 minutes, checking for doneness after 20 minutes. The cake should bounce back when you touch it lightly with your finger tips and should also pull away slightly from the sides of the pan.

10.   Prepare a kitchen towel by sprinkling entire surface with sifted powdered sugar. Turn cake out onto the towel and remove the waxed paper. Roll the cake up in the towel lengthwise, jelly-roll fashion, and let it cool this way.

B. Make the frosting, then fill and frost the cake.

Chocolate Mocha Cream Filling and Frosting:

1/2 c.	unsweetened cocoa
3/4 c.	sugar
2 tsp.	instant coffee
2 tsp.	butter, softened
1/4 c.	hot water
1/2 tsp.	vanilla extract
1/2 tsp.	almond extract
2 c.	heavy cream

Powdered chocolate, for garnish
Powdered sugar, for garnish

1.   Add all ingredients except powdered chocolate and powdered sugar to a mixing bowl in order listed above, mixing with a whip or electric beater as you add, but do not beat vigorously yet. Chill, covered, for 1 hour or more.

2.   When ready to fill cake, whip mixture until it is very thick and light chocolate color. This chocolate butter cream gets very thick (like frosting), and the whole beating process will take about 10 minutes.

3.   Place the rolled-up cake on a serving platter, using the towel as a sling for support. Then unroll the cake and fill with part of the filling to within 1" of the edges. Roll up the cake, taking away the towel slowly so that the Yule log now sits in the center of the serving platter, seam side down.

4.   Use the remaining frosting to frost the whole outside of the log. At this point, don't worry how perfect it looks because it will be camouflaged with decorations.

5. Cut off about 1 inch from each end of the log diagonally. Place these atop the log to resemble branch stumps and frost these as well.

6. Using a fork, make lines in the butter cream to resemble wood bark. With a small strainer, sprinkle with a little powdered chocolate (to resemble earth) and powdered sugar (to resemble snow).

C. Make the meringue decorations and complete the dessert.

Meringue Mushrooms:

1	large egg white, at room temperature
	Dash salt
1/3 c.	sugar

1. Preheat oven to 250 degrees. In a bowl, beat egg white and salt until frothy, gradually add sugar, and beat until very stiff. Spoon into a pastry bag.

2. Pipe mixture onto a cookie sheet lined with plain brown paper (a grocery bag will do.) Pipe buttons and stems separately. Bake for about 30 minutes, or until tan in color and dry. Let cool completely.

3. Assemble by dipping the stems into melted butter and pressing them into the "buttons."

4. To finish the dessert, place the mushrooms around the Yule log.

5. Chill the log well. Serve in 1-inch-thick slices. Refrigerate the decorated cake for 24 hours, or freeze without the meringue mushrooms, powdered chocolate, and powdered sugar for up to one month. If frozen, bring out of freezer and let stand in the refrigerator for 3 hours to defrost before decorating and serving.

Special Celebration #5:

A Christmas Homecoming Dinner

Bombay Cheese Pâté
Red and Green Vegetable Salad
Roast Turkey with Cornbread Stuffing
Cranberry Chutney
Mashed potatoes and Gravy
Puréed Peas in Mushroom Caps
Pumpkin Bread Pudding with Caramel Cream

Christmas or a winter break makes a wonderful opportunity to be purposely merry, to give to others, and to get together with seldom-seen friends and relatives. For those of us who practice different religious faiths, this time can bring us all together. It is a time to remember to respect each other's beliefs, and to forgive hurts that we feel have been committed to us. With forgiveness comes a lightening of our burdens and a deepening of our spirit. Why not choose to celebrate the season together, rather than separately? What better time to celebrate the miracle of unity than during the common pause we take before beginning the labors of a new year.

Bombay Cheese Pâté

This unusual cheese ball freezes well when wrapped tightly in several layers of plastic wrap and then put in a plastic bag, so you can make it ahead of time.

Makes about 2 cups.

11 oz.	cream cheese, softened
3 Tbs.	raisins, chopped
3 Tbs.	sour cream
3 Tbs.	curry powder
3/4 c.	cocktail peanuts
1/2 lb.	cooked, crisp bacon, crumbled
1/2 c.	chopped green onions
1 c.	chutney
	Finely grated, unsweetened coconut

1. Mix together all of the ingredients, reserving half of the chutney and the coconut. DO NOT USE A MIXER.
2. Form into one or two balls. Refrigerate.
3. Frost with chutney and sprinkle liberally with finely toasted and grated coconut.
4. Serve with your favorite crackers.

"May Christmas be truly a rebirth of love, light and wonder.

May the coming year be a year of joy and grace, healing us all."

— Anonymous

Red and Green Vegetable Salad

I like to prepare this for the holidays, too, because it can be made the day ahead and all you have to do is put it on the table to be served.

Serves 10.

1 c.	cherry tomatoes, halved
2 pts.	Brussels sprouts

Dressing:

1/2 c.	canola oil
1-1/2 oz.	cider vinegar
1 tsp.	salt
1	clove garlic, minced
1 Tbs.	minced green onions
1 Tbs.	minced red pepper
1 Tbs.	minced fresh Italian parsley
2 drops	Tabasco sauce

1. Cook Brussels sprouts al dente — i.e., still firm, about 10 minutes. Drain, cool, and cut them in half.
2. Place in a bowl with the halved cherry tomatoes.
3. Make dressing: Combine dressing ingredients in screw-top jar and shake well. Pour over the vegetables. Marinate in refrigerator for at least 5 hours, stirring occasionally.
4. To serve, place in a clear glass bowl or line a platter with crisp greens and pile the salad on the greens.

Roast Turkey with Cornbread Stuffing

This is my family's traditional favorite.

Serves 10 to 12.

Cornbread, for the stuffing:

1 c.	yellow cornmeal
1 c.	unbleached flour
3 tsp.	baking powder
1 tsp.	salt
1 c.	milk
1/4 c.	shortening, melted and cooled
1	large egg

1. Make the cornbread 1 to 2 days beforehand so it can dry out. Preheat oven to 425 degrees. Grease a square pan, 8x8x2 or 9x9x2 inches.
2. Blend all ingredients together in a bowl only about 1 minute; then pour into the prepared pan and bake for 20 to 25 minutes. Test bread with a skewer inserted into the center. If it comes out clean, the cornbread is done.
3. Cool cornbread, then cover well with plastic wrap and refrigerate until ready to make the stuffing.

Stuffing (also see "My Way"):

1/4 c.	butter
3 Tbs.	minced fresh Italian parsley
1/2	onion, chopped
1 c.	chopped celery
2	large eggs
3 c.	cornbread, cubed
1-1/4 c.	plain, toasted bread cubes
3/4 tsp.	salt
2 tsp.	dried sage
1/2 tsp.	dried thyme
1 tsp.	dried savory
1 tsp.	dried marjoram
	Freshly ground black pepper to taste
	Extra chicken stock if needed

1. Melt butter in pan and sauté parsley, onions, and celery till tender. Set aside.
2. Remove cornbread from refrigerator and cut into small cubes.

My Way:

I usually end up making a double recipe of the stuffing.

3. In a large bowl, beat the eggs. Add cubed cornbread and all other seasonings and mix well.

4. Add the plain, toasted bread cubes and sautéed vegetables and mix again. If stuffing is too dry, add some chicken stock, but don't be tempted to add too much or the stuffing will be soggy. Taste for seasoning, and add more if necessary. You may make this dressing ahead to this point and refrigerate overnight, but DO NOT stuff the turkey until you are ready to roast it.

Turkey:

	Salt and freshly ground black pepper to taste
1	clove garlic, crushed
1/2 tsp.	thyme
1	fresh turkey, washed, dried, and giblets removed
1/4 c.	oil
	Double piece cheesecloth

1. Preheat oven to 425 degrees. Make a paste of the salt, pepper, garlic, and thyme and rub it inside and over the bird. Stuff some of the stuffing mixture into the bird and truss it. (Place rest of dressing into an oiled, oven-proof casserole dish and bake for 30 to 40 minutes at 350 degrees just before serving.)

2. Place the turkey on a rack over a roasting pan. Dip the cheesecloth in the oil and drape it gently over the turkey. This bastes the turkey so that you don't have to.

3. Bake at 425 degrees for 30 minutes. Reduce heat to 325 degrees and bake approximately 3-1/2 hours for a 10- to 14-lb. bird. I always use a thermometer inserted into the deepest part of the bird around the thigh, being careful so that the thermometer does not touch the bone. The bird is done when the thermometer reads 170 degrees.

Cranberry Chutney

Makes about 4 cups.

1 c.	water
4 c.	fresh cranberries
1 c.	golden raisins
2 c.	sugar
1/2 tsp.	cinnamon
1/4 tsp.	allspice
1 tsp.	minced fresh ginger, or 1/2 tsp. powdered
1/4 tsp.	salt
1 small can	crushed pineapple, drained

1. Combine water, cranberries, raisins, sugar, spices, and salt in a large saucepan.
2. Mix well and cook over medium heat till cranberries pop and mixture begins to thicken, about 20 minutes.
3. Stir in drained pineapple. Continue cooking for 20 minutes longer or till sauce has reached desired thickness.
4. Cool and store in refrigerator for up to 2 weeks. Can be preserved. Also good with chicken, duck, or fish.

"Creative is what we are when you take the fear away."

— Terry Louise Fisher

Mashed Potatoes and Gravy

Respecting foods from our past is part of cooking with spirit. The loving energy used in preparing these foods and serving them to family and friends enriches everyone's spirit.

Serves 6 to 8.

Mashed Potatoes:

2 lbs.	potatoes
5 Tbs.	butter
1/3 c.	milk (or more)
	Salt and white pepper to taste

1. Cook the peeled and quartered potatoes in boiling, salted water until tender, then drain.
2. Add the butter, some of the milk, and salt and white pepper to taste. Crush with a potato masher until potatoes are light and fluffy, adding more milk, salt, and pepper as required.

Giblet Gravy:

4 c.	canned or fresh chicken stock
	Giblets from the turkey, all except for the liver, which you can discard
2	carrots, scrubbed and cut into small chunks
1	large onion, peeled and cut into large chunks
2	celery ribs plus the leaves, washed and cut into large chunks
1	bay leaf
1/2 tsp.	thyme
4 sprigs	fresh Italian parsley
1/2 tsp.	salt, or to taste
6 to 8	black peppercorns
1/2 c.	Wondra "instant" flour mixed with 1/2 c. water (Wondra is superior in sauces to all-purpose flour, as it does not "lump up")

1. Place the chicken stock, giblets, vegetables, and herbs, salt, and peppercorns in a large pot and bring to a boil. You may also add the discarded mushroom stems from the from the Puréed Peas in Mushroom Caps to this. Simmer on the stove for at least 45 minutes, then let stand to cool.

2. When cool, strain the broth, pressing hard on the vegetables to extract all of the flavorful juice. Discard the vegetables.

3. Put the gravy stock back into the pot and slowly add the flour/water mixture, stirring constantly. Add just enough to thicken the sauce to your liking. You may not need to use all of the flour/water mixture.

4. Simmer for 15 to 20 minutes before serving. You may double this recipe if necessary.

"Yesterday I dared to struggle. Today I dare to win."

— Anonymous

Puréed Peas in Mushroom Caps

These are a Christmas vegetable tradition in my family. They may be prepared, frozen, and then baked when ready to serve.

Serves 8 to 12.

2 pkgs.	frozen peas, cooked very briefly in the microwave and then drained (they should still be very green in color) (10-oz. pkg.)
4 Tbs.	butter
2 Tbs.	flour
2 Tbs.	cream
2 Tbs.	salt
1/8 tsp.	white pepper
24 large	mushroom caps, stems removed and discarded, caps cleaned thoroughly and a small part of the center scooped out
3 Tbs.	melted butter

1. Preheat oven to 400 degrees. Purée the cooked peas in the food processor.
2. Melt 4 Tbs. of the butter and stir in the flour. Cook till lightly browned, stirring constantly. Remove from heat and stir in the cream.
3. Add puréed peas, salt, and pepper. Blend well.
4. Place the mushrooms on a greased cookie sheet and spoon some of the puréed peas into each mushroom cap.
5. Drizzle the 3 Tbs. melted butter over them and bake for 10 minutes. Serve immediately.

Pumpkin Bread Pudding with Caramel Cream

Serves 10 to 12.

4 c.	diced brioche bread
1/4 c.	butter, melted
2 c.	milk
2 c.	heavy cream
6	large eggs
2/3 c.	sugar
2 c.	canned pumpkin purée
2 Tbs.	dark molasses
2 tsp.	vanilla extract
2 tsp.	ground ginger
2 tsp.	cinnamon

1. Preheat oven to 350 degrees.
2. Place diced brioche on a baking tray, sprinkle with melted butter, and toast lightly in oven for 15 minutes.
3. Butter an oven-proof baking dish (approximately 8x12x3 inches deep) and place the brioche in the bottom of the dish.
4. In a small saucepan, heat milk and cream together to almost the boiling point.
5. In a bowl, whisk together eggs, sugar, pumpkin purée, molasses, vanilla, and spices. Add hot milk mixture, whisk again, then pour the mixture over the bread. Let stand for 20 minutes, until brioche has absorbed the liquid.
6. Place the pudding in a larger dish or pan with high sides. Fill the large pan halfway with boiling water. Bake the pudding in the water bath for 30 to 40 minutes until the center is set — test it with a knife. It should be firm but moist.
7. Serve with Caramel Cream.

Caramel Cream:

3/4 c.	sugar
1-1/2 c.	heavy cream
8 oz.	mascarpone cheese

"I am loved. You are loved. The real hunger is for love, so open your heart and give it now."

1. In a saucepan, cook sugar over low heat, stirring with a fork till dissolved. It will begin to caramelize. When pale brown, remove from heat and slowly add 3 Tbs. of the heavy cream, being careful not to be spattered with the hot sugar.

2. Return to low heat and stir for 15 seconds. Remove from heat and allow to cool.

3. In a mixing bowl, whisk together the remaining cream with the mascarpone till smooth. Add the cooled caramel mixture and continue to whisk till the cream thickens. Refrigerate until ready to use. Reheat slowly, but do not boil.

Afterword

Surely, we eat to live, but there is more to the dining ritual than simple sustenance. Sometimes my friends, especially new ones, are intimidated to ask me over for dinner. I tell them, "Look, serve me a hotdog and canned beans! Okay, that may be a little extreme, but the reason I come for dinner is to see you." Ultimately, that's what it's all about: We have created the sharing of food at dinners or lunches or picnics, but the real purpose of these gatherings is to connect with people we love, people who are fun to be with, people who enhance our lives — people who excite us in some way. It's not about the food, it's about the people.

As you set out to make this realization for yourself, I wish you the true joy that comes from cooking with spirit and sharing the fruits of your labors with the people you love.

— D.J.

Index

About the Author

Darlene Jones was born in Gravelbourg, Saskatchewan, Canada, and now lives, cooks, teaches, and learns in Portland, Oregon. As a teacher of gourmet cooking for twenty-five years, she is an adept presenter/speaker in the areas of cooking, entertaining, and self-development.

Self-taught from the age of sixteen, Ms. Jones went on to study the culinary arts with nationally recognized teachers, including workshops with chef James Beard and seminars at Essalon Institute in Big Sur, California; and to study spirituality with Leslie Temple Thurston and many other guides and teachers, as well as on a personal level for thirty years. Leadership and public relations expertise came with a return to college; development of the Darlene Jones International School of Cooking; and world travel to Europe, Australia, Scandinavia, the Soviet Union, the Middle East, Asia, the Caribbean, Mexico and the Hawaiian Islands. A sharp sense of style and diverse organizational skills were sharpened through work in interior design, fashion design, and events coordination.

When she is not teaching or meditating, Ms. Jones enjoys hiking, gardening, skiing, boating, and appreciating art, opera, and literature. She continues her lifelong study of food, history, geography, psychology, and spirituality. Still, she asserts, "I feel like I'm in kindergarten and I'm just beginning."

To order additional copies of

Cooking with Spirit

Contact:
Lang Publishing
6663 S.W. Beaverton Hillsdale Highway #105
Portland, Oregon 97225

E-mail: darlene@darlenejones.com

Web site: www.cookingwithspirit.com

Or:
Check your local book store.